To Elvis,

You're Aunt Sarah told me that you like to invest in the stock market. Read my 8th & 9th inning and the Wall Street Journal or other financial books to help educate you.

<u>Warren Buffett Quotes</u>:

" Price is what you pay. Value is what you get"

" Rule #1: Never lose money, Rule #2: " Never forget Rule #1"

" Never invest in a business you can't understand"

" If a business does well, the stock (eventually) follows"

" It takes 20 years to build a reputation and 5 minutes to ruin it, if you think about it, you'll do things differently"

Happy Trading,
Lenny Sika

NINE INNINGS

LIFE LESSONS LEARNED

Practical advice by a father, baseball coach, and financial advisor to help young student athletes, and their parents become more confident, mentally strong, positive, street smart, money focused, successful, and well balanced in school, sports, work and life.

LENNY SILVA

"**An Inspirational and Motivational book that will change your life**"
Ken Ryan-Boston Red Sox

iUniverse, Inc.
New York Bloomington

Nine Innings
Life Lessons Learned

Copyright © 2010 by Lenny Silva

All rights reserved. No part of this book may be used or reproduced by any means, graphic, electronic, or mechanical, including photocopying, recording, taping or by any information storage retrieval system without the written permission of the publisher except in the case of brief quotations embodied in critical articles and reviews.

The views expressed in this work are solely those of the author and do not necessarily reflect the views of the publisher, and the publisher hereby disclaims any responsibility for them.

This publication is designed to provide practical advice and information in regard to the subject matter covered. It is published with the understanding that the Author is not engaged in rendering legal, accounting, medical or any other professional service. If legal advice or other professional advice, including financial, is required, seek a competent professional. The holder of this book expressly releases and holds harmless the Author from any and all liability, loss, damage, costs, claims and/or causes of actions arising from the purchase of this book.

iUniverse books may be ordered through booksellers or by contacting:

iUniverse
1663 Liberty Drive
Bloomington, IN 47403
www.iuniverse.com
1-800-Authors (1-800-288-4677)

Because of the dynamic nature of the Internet, any Web addresses or links contained in this book may have changed since publication and may no longer be valid.

ISBN: 978-1-4502-3963-9 (sc)
ISBN: 978-1-4502-3962-2 (dj)
ISBN: 978-1-4502-3961-5 (ebk)

Library of Congress Control Number: 2010908943

Printed in the United States of America

iUniverse rev. date: 6/21/2010

This book is dedicated to my sons Jacob and Joshua. You both are an inspiration to me and with confidence in yourselves anything is possible. Your mother and father will love you forever and we support your journeys in life. We are so proud of you both so dream big and just go for it.

Contents

Spring Training
    Introduction . . . . *ix*

First Inning
    Street Smart *1*

Second Inning
    Dream Car By Len Zen *19*

Third Inning
    Jacob Becomes Mentally Tough and Learns About The Four C's . . *35*

Fourth Inning
    Joshua Stops Procrastinating *57*

Fifth Inning
    Understanding the Importance of Being a Good Student Athlete . . *73*

Sixth Inning
    Anxiety in Baseball and Life *87*

Seventh Inning
    Health is Wealth *103*

Eighth Inning
    Understanding the Importance of Money and Investing *121*

Ninth Inning
    Control Your Debt and Spending Habits *135*

Extra Innings
    Sample of a Monthly Budget Form: *153*
    Instructions to Balance Your Checkbook: *155*
    Goal Setting Workshop: *159*
    Building Dynamic Credit: *161*
    Financial Investment Guide: *165*
    Financial Documents Archive Checklist: *169*
    Acknowledgments: *173*

Playoffs
About the Author *181*

Spring Training

Introduction

I was fortunate enough to grow up with a loving mother and father, along with two sisters and a younger brother. It was a happy household and busy time as we all tried to find our way in this game we call life. It was a wonderful time and I got my first job as a stock boy at our local liquor store.

I was thirteen and walked fifteen minutes to work every Saturday. I made fifteen dollars working four hours every Saturday afternoon stocking shelves. I became quite successful helping customers carry their bags to their cars. The customers appreciated the extra effort and they would reward me with a tip. My boss was impressed as it was my idea, and he thought it would help to increase our sales because the customers began telling all their friends who then decided to do their shopping at our store.

Life Lesson *Remember to treat customers the way you like to be treated because the customers will tell their friends and word of mouth advertising is priceless.*

This first job taught me much about responsibility and the importance of treating people with respect. I enjoyed my time working and earning my first paycheck even though it was under the table. This is also the first time I began to start thinking about where I would be ten years from now.

Life lesson *Stand up straight, shake hands firmly, look your customer, boss, friends and people with authority in the eye when communicating.*

I realized that ten years from now I would be twenty-three years old and would be living someplace in this world and it would only make my life easier if I had a few bucks saved up. I began to save for my future at the age of thirteen by setting both short-term and long- term goals.

Life Lesson *Planning for your future requires you to write down your goals and then review frequently, and work towards reaching them. This behavior learned at an early age helped shape my life as an adult.*

I always think about where will I be ten years from now and ask that all of you who are reading this start doing the same thing. God willing, we all will be living somewhere on this earth ten years from now. If you want to improve your life and accomplish all of your dreams, planning and saving, along with hard work will bring you closer to reaching your goals. Ten years goes by very fast so let's get going.

I still remember when my parents drove me to the local bank and helped me open my first savings account. Saving money for me became an obsession and I would put away almost every dollar that I earned. I would get so excited watching my money grow. Even though my account only earned a little interest, it taught me a valuable lesson about how money can grow by compounding. I would always continue to try and save and invest my money, even up to the present day.

Life Lesson *It is important to have a monthly budget and control your spending. If you can't pay off your credit bill in full each month then don't use it. A penny saved is truly a penny earned.*

I continued to work all through high school. At the age of fifteen, I got a better paying job working as an usher at the local movie theater. I still remember the interview. I was so proud talking about my first job and the great customer service I provided. This was a fun job. Not only did I earn more money, I got to watch all the movies and eat popcorn for free.

Life Lesson *Find a job you love and look at all the benefits provided because life is short so enjoy it. I was now earning more money and spending less. If you spend less you can save more.*

I managed to have some fun by playing both baseball and basketball. These are two sports that I loved. I had earned a reputation in our town as a good athlete. I was considered an outstanding baseball player, having the skills to pitch and play shortstop.

During my Little League career, I did most of the pitching and I was fortunate enough to throw several no-hitters throughout the regular season, as well as in our all-star tournaments. No kidding, almost every time I pitched, it was a no-hitter.

At the age of thirteen, I was the number one draft choice in baseball having moved up from the Little League fields to the big ninety-foot diamond. The team manager had a son who was older and was a pitcher. I was told that I could help the team by playing shortstop full time and was asked to make this sacrifice. Always putting the team first, I said yes and my pitching days were behind me.

Life Lesson *There is no letter I in the word team, but it is in the word win, so make a personal sacrifice and contribute to your team in order to win.*

I learned everything that I could about playing the position of shortstop. I would constantly watch the shortstop for the Boston Red Sox. You can learn so much by watching professional athletes, from the way they move to the ball and how they get their body aligned to make accurate throws.

In high school, my skills as a shortstop only got better. I got bigger and more confident playing the position. God had blessed me with blazing speed and our high school baseball coach had only one set of sliding pants and they were reserved for me. In my senior year of high school, we had an extra game scheduled one week. Our team was short a pitcher, so my coach asked me if I could start the game and pitch. I said "No problem" and it was the only game that I pitched during my four years in high school. This is the first game that I had pitched since I was twelve and in Little League. I threw a **no hitter**. I walked the opposing teams clean up hitter four times and we won the game.

Life Lesson *Remember past successes you achieved as a recording in your mind and then retrieve them when necessary to exceed expectations. This technique works really well for golf, especially right after hitting a good shot.*

I also became a stand out player on my high school basketball team. I would use my speed and quick hands to steal the ball from my opponent and make the lay up. I would average five steals per game, which quickly turned into ten points for my team. I had fun playing basketball and loved playing defense. I enjoyed taking my opponent full court baseline to baseline making it difficult for him to get the ball over half court in the **ten seconds allowed**.

Life lesson *If everyone would just take ten seconds to think before acting in certain situations, you may protect yourself from harm or from getting into trouble. Every decision that you make and the action that you take should lead to a positive outcome for you. If it does not then refrain from doing it because in the end you only end up hurting yourself.*

I was feeling great during high school. I excelled in athletics and was saving lots of money, but I was falling way behind in the classroom. I did not take my schoolwork seriously and it is something that I regret the most as I look back. My parents and teachers would always tell me that getting good grades is the most important thing and is the key to the future, especially if you want to go to college.

Oops, unfortunately college was not something that I wrote down as one of my goals when I was thirteen. I had no idea what a student athlete was all about. I got a perfect score of 100 percent in athletics and a failing score on the academic half of that equation.

Hey, I was only thirteen at the time when I set my short and long-term goals so let's give a kid a break. Nobody said I was perfect.

Life lesson *We all make mistakes. You can turn a loss into a win by learning something from it.*

At the age of thirteen, I forgot to write down my goal to attend college. It is never too late to make a change. With the help of my high school guidance counselor and head baseball coach for Rhode Island College, that possibility became a reality.

Life lesson *Ask for help and use all the resources available to you in an effort to win and succeed in the classroom, athletics, work and life.*

I applied to Rhode Island College in 1983 and was accepted with good references from the head baseball coach at RIC and my high school guidance counselor. I was the first child on both my parents' side of the family to attend college. No pressure here! I still remember the first day driving through the campus with my dad. I was terrified about going to college and not having one friend at the school. My dad said the first day is always the hardest and then after that you become aware of your surroundings and it would get easier. He was right, because on the first day the head baseball coach had a baseball team meeting and I met twenty- five new friends. After that first day, we would all meet for lunch every day and having our own table was cool. The ladies were very impressed.

Life Lesson *Change is always uncomfortable at first, but remain positive. Before you know it you will adjust and settle in. You will become familiar with your surroundings.*

The next few weeks in college were hard. You had to make sure you got to class on time and with all the freedom to roam, you had to be disciplined and stay focused on studying. Not for me. Remember, I was that kid who had blown off studying in high school, and I thought that I could do the same thing in college. After my first semester, I was just passing my courses, and the head baseball coach called me into his office. He said that if I don't maintain a B average I could not play baseball. I was amazed and hit with the reality that schoolwork was important and I had to get it done. I loved playing baseball and now after making the starting line up as a freshman, realized I was blowing it because of bad grades.

Life lesson. *If, you love a sport then let that motivate you to do well in school. Today, if you're getting bad grades they won't let you play sports. It is important to have balance and with a little effort in school you can have it all.*

I made a choice and committed myself to increasing my study time to get better grades in the classroom. I was working a full-time job, paying my way through college, playing baseball, studying hard trying to get my grades up, and trying to have a social life entertaining the ladies all at the same time. I was trying to juggle these four areas in my life and trying to manage them successfully. It was not easy, but if you stay focused and organized you can manage everything.

Life lesson. *Time management skills are very important. You can make it all work if you focus and use your time wisely. It is important to prioritize and work daily to reach your goals. Keep a schedule and list all activities to stay organized.*

I am proud to tell you that I graduated from Rhode Island College in 1987 with a B average and earned my Bachelor of Science degree in Marketing / Management. I also earned some outstanding athletic awards during my four-year college baseball career and met the woman of my dreams.

In February 2005, I was selected as a member of Rhode Island College's **All 75th Anniversary Men's Baseball team**. A collegiate committee reviews the qualifications of every student athlete who had been a member of the college baseball team over the past 75 years. As you can imagine, the list was remarkable and the biographies on all the finalists for the 75th anniversary team were quite impressive. There were thousands of outstanding student athletes over this seventy-five year period. I was one of only nineteen players selected to represent this All-75th anniversary baseball team. I was a stand out shortstop that had compiled an impressive set of records. In May of 2008, I was inducted into Rhode Island College **Athletic Hall Of Fame**. I played in 101 career baseball games, totaling 130 hits, and had a .362 career batting average, which are top 5 all time in both categories. I scored 95 runs, with 55 runs batted in, 20 doubles, five triples and ten home runs. I am the college all time leader with 64 stolen bases a record that I still hold today.

Well, I was right and I did make it to the age of twenty-one and became the first child in my entire family to graduate from college. My mom and dad were so proud as nobody on either side of the family had ever accomplished such a goal. I looked back at those ten years and realized how much I actually accomplished.

I held my first job at the age of thirteen, advanced into a better paying job by the age of fifteen and managed to graduate from high school. I went to college while working full time to pay for it. I finished with a collegiate Hall of Fame baseball career, and earned a Bachelor of Science degree from Rhode Island College. I also found time to meet the woman of my dreams. During my hall of fame speech I ended it by saying come to Rhode Island College, where you can earn a quality education, compete in athletics, and meet your spouse. Everyone laughed, the President of the school loved it and said that would make a good commercial promoting the college. I was pleased to be fortunate to accomplish so much while in college and I got out all that I could from my years in college.

Life Lesson: *It can be a tough decision which college you want to attend especially if you're an athlete and schools are recruiting you. Step back and think about all that you accomplished in high school. If you agree that you got everything you could out of high school excelling both in the classroom, and on the athletic fields then imagine yourself doing the same in college? Challenge yourself for this next step and it can become another four years of fun. Only 2 percent of people are considered a college student athlete, the other 98 percent are students.*

It is very important to set both short and long-term goals for yourself. I think we all should look back at our last ten years to reflect on our accomplishments. I am sure you will find something positive in your life that happened or contributions that you made to either your family or community. You can look back at these accomplishments and contributions to help motivate yourself and set new goals for the next ten years. I know you will be someplace in this world. When I was twenty-one years old, I started setting my short and long-term goals for the next ten years, knowing that I would make it to the age of thirty-one. I was now a college graduate I needed to raise the bar and aim higher.

Life Lesson: *Take the time to reflect on your accomplishments and challenge yourself. Once you become complacent it will lead to laziness and you are all better then that. Set your goals high and work hard to achieve them and feel proud of your accomplishment. Never get frustrated if you fall short and remain positive in all that you do.*

Lenny Silva

I wanted to pursue my baseball career and wanted to turn professional. I was invited to a professional baseball tryout in the summer of 1987. I was one of about 100 players from the New York and New England region. It was a great experience. The regional scout running the tryout had been following me during the four years I played in college.

I did very well in the tryout and was the only player selected to fill out my personal information card for the professional baseball scout. This is a card with your name, address and home phone numbers. The scout said that he had another tryout later that week and would be contacting me soon to discuss options to advance my career and turn pro. A week went by with no phone call. I started to wonder if he would actually call or if he was just telling me a story and the opportunity would not present itself. The phone rang eight days after the tryout and it was the scout. He explained that he ran three more tryouts and looked at hundreds of players and I was the only one worthy of this phone call.

He offered me an opportunity to play professional baseball. I asked the scout about a signing bonus and my annual salary. I had just graduated from college and thought I would try out the new negotiating skills that I learned in school. Big mistake because I actually turned the scout right off. He told me that they were getting shortstops a dime a dozen from the Dominican Republic for free. They were looking for ballplayers who didn't care about money but love the game. I told him that I did love the game and was willing to work hard. I was only trying to get some information about money so I could earn enough to live. The scout said that he would think it over and call me back. He called back and explained that the whole organization would be heading into the direction of selecting ballplayers from the Dominican Republic.

He would go on to say that he followed my entire college career. He was impressed with my speed, arm, glove, and hitting for both power and high average. He felt badly, but the organization decided to make this move with international players. I told him that I was only asking about a higher signing bonus and if they were not willing to pay, it was not a problem on my part. Well, I basically blew the whole deal. I did not handle myself in this situation very well over the phone. I just kept sticking my foot in my mouth and everything I said just came across the wrong way.

Life Lesson *God gave you two ears and one mouth for a reason. You learn more by listening then talking. We all can benefit from listening more and talking less.*

The next week, I was on a bus with a local amateur baseball team and traveled to Moncton, Canada for a two-week baseball tournament. We played against some of the best teams in the country who had former professional baseball greats playing for them. It was a great experience to get a taste of the baseball life, traveling and playing baseball every day. I played exceptionally well during this time but was never approached by any other scouts. I returned home and decided to move on with my life and began a career in the financial services industry. I had hung up my spikes and put my dreams of becoming a professional baseball player away.

Life Lesson *Don't put all your eggs in one basket. It was a good thing that I studied and earned my college degree because I did not become a professional baseball player.*

I landed a great full-time job and after dating my dream girl for six years, I asked her to marry me. We married on August 22, 1992. A year later, we had our first son and four years after that we had our second son. Wow, I was now thirty-one years old and I couldn't believe all that had happened during this ten-year span. I was offered a professional baseball contract, got married, bought my first house, began a successful career in finance and had two healthy baby boys. I think that raising the bar and hitting these goals over this ten-year period was very exciting. It was time to set new goals for the next ten years because I would be forty-one years old and living somewhere in this world. I needed to plan my work and work my plan to reach new heights.

Over the next ten years, I wanted to become more active in my community and become a trusted mentor not only to my two sons, but also to any other child who needed help and guidance. I became the president of my town's Little League program. It was a big responsibility, but it was worth it, especially when they throw out the first pitch each season. It is great watching all the kids play baseball and very satisfying knowing you helped to make that experience possible for the children in your community. Our board of directors for baseball also set goals just like we all need to do as individuals. We set out to repair all the fields, making them safer to play. In 2007, we completed the construction of a new Little League field. This was a great accomplishment for our board and the kids would benefit from this new field for generations to come.

Life Lesson *Become a volunteer and always remember to give back to your community. Help share the gifts that you may have to others who could benefit from it.*

I turned forty-one years old. When looking back, I felt very happy with all that had been accomplished. I think you all get the point and understand the importance to start thinking about your future. The whole world can be yours if you just take some time and think about what you would like to do and then go for it. I enjoy baseball and even though I never signed a professional baseball contract, I did accomplish much. I had a Hall of Fame college career and made new friends for life.

We all should look back at our past ten years and reflect on our accomplishments. If you did not meet all of your expectations then do not let this deter you. Write them down as goals for you to work toward over the next ten years.

I am a Boston Fan and enjoy watching all four of our sports teams: the New England Patriots, Boston Red Sox, Boston Celtics and the Boston Bruins. Let's take a look back over the past ten years and examine what they have accomplished as organizations.

The Patriots won three super bowls, the Red Sox won two championships, Celtics added one more championship and the Bruins are improving. I am sure that these four organizations are writing down their short and long-term goals over the next ten years and I ask that you do the same.

The next nine chapters in this book are written for you and the materials are techniques to help you become mentally stronger and more focused. They are life lessons learned and maybe something that you read in this book will help you stay safe, become more confident, courageous, and successful in school, sports, work and life.

We all love to go to a baseball game so enjoy the next nine chapters of the book, which coincide with ***nine innings*** of a baseball game. Make sure that you stay for the ***extra innings*** and read all six of those one-page chapters, which offer you a skill-building workshop. Remember that we can choose our attitude, so try and wake up everyday with energy and have confidence in all that you do. Stay positive and never give up on your goals as your journey in life continues. You will find success in all that you attempt to accomplish, because you must believe in order to achieve.

I believe in all of you and have faith that you will succeed and become a trusted mentor or advisor to another that may need your help. The greatest gift of all is to share your knowledge and talents with all those who can benefit from it. I am offering my fatherly advice that hopefully will help you to become more confident, street smart, mentally strong, positive, focused and successful. I can only share the information with you and in the end it is up to you to make it work in your life. The **four C's** to greatness are *Confidence, Courage, Competitiveness,* and *Continued improvement and you will learn all about these in the book.* You are great young adults and you are our leaders of tomorrow. You can help yourself and others by always being considerate, compassionate, trusting, honest, and responsible. I am inspired by all of you and look forward to your greatness.

Life Lesson: *Always treat people the way that you would like to be treated. Live and let live because we all are not perfect and make mistakes. Only GOD can judge so remember the old saying that people who live in glass houses should not throw stones.*

First Inning

Street Smart

As athletes playing baseball, we are all taught about the importance of **being prepared**. I still remember advice my little league coach gave the boys and girls on my team. While playing defense, it is important to know what you're going to do with the baseball prior to it being hit your way. I used that advice throughout my entire baseball career, including college. It is simple advice and an important action principle when playing defense.

The coach would explain that prior to our pitcher delivering the pitch, understand the game situation and run your options through your mind. This game moves so quickly and you really don't have time to think. We only have time to react and make a play. Having a high baseball IQ and using your instincts separates the good from the great players of the game.

As a shortstop-playing defense, we have so many options when making a play to get an out. It is very important to always be thinking and prepared to make a play before the ball is hit our way. I would run all the options through my mind prior to the pitch being thrown. If the opponent had runners on first and second base with nobody out, here are some options a player at shortstop could be thinking about:

1. If the ball is hit to my right in the hole near third base, I could throw it to the third baseman for a force play, or I

could pivot and throw to second base for a possible double play. I would say to my third baseman "If the ball goes here, be ready because I may be coming to you for the force out." Communicating with teammates was crucial.

2. If it was a slow bounding ball hit right to me, then I would charge it, catching the ground ball off the infield grass, throwing it to first base, getting one out.

3. If the ball is hit to my left, then I could catch the ball, tag second base, and throw it to first for a double play.

These three types of scenarios would run through my mind prior to the pitcher delivering the pitch. You must always be prepared and understand what you are going to do with the baseball prior to it being hit your way so you increase the chance that you will make the right choice and play for your team. Become a highly intelligent athlete and this action principle of being prepared can be applied to any sport you love to play as it can help both boys and girls become more successful in athletics.

In life it is so important to always be prepared. If we take what you learned from the game of baseball and applied that same technique to your life then maybe you could avoid a dangerous situation or get to safety if you are ever thrust into one.

Life Lesson: *Try to be prepared and always expect the unexpected.*

In life, I call this being **street smart**. A **street smart** person is somebody who is prepared has some basic knowledge and a cool head when faced with danger. A person who thinks ahead and has good instincts remaining calm may have an increased chance to survive a dangerous situation that may come up unexpectedly.

Being street smart is a catch phrase to help the child become more mentally tough and focused. It allows you to take action when your natural survival instincts are sending you warning bells. We all need to be aware of our surroundings and thinking about options if we are ever faced with danger. We can react more quickly than people who are not prepared. All of us have survival instincts and we sometimes refer to them as gut feelings. This is a warning signal to your brain that something does not feel right and you don't want to ignore it.

If you do experience this type of feeling, then understand that you about to enter into a dangerous situation and it is important to remain calm and begin to look around for options and ways to flee the area to safety.

As a parent, we try to educate our children and prepare them to avoid talking to strangers and anyone who may have bad intentions towards them. If your child feels uncomfortable or threatened, then they need to take action. We try to protect our children from danger but we cannot always be there with them. It comes down to the child to make the right choices.

Unfortunately, it is not that easy to have your child just be aware of strangers. In the majority of violent cases against children, they involve someone the parent or child may know and trust. We need to educate our children of all ages about being safe and their right to protect themselves from harm.

What is a child to do? What is a parent to do? As a parent, we want to teach and protect them from uncomfortable situations and anyone who may pose a threat to their safety. This includes strangers and people whom they may know and trust. We must make the child aware that their safety comes first. Once the situation is detected as dangerous, you must take action to get yourself to safety and be vigilant in your efforts to do so. Being prepared, keeping a cool head and using basic knowledge are all traits to help you get to safety while dealing with the pressure of any traumatic event that may be occurring.

I teach my boys that out in the world, safety is much more important than having good manners. We all want our kids to have good manners and be polite by saying please and thank you. In the event of an unexpected danger, they must seek help and get away.

If any child feels uncomfortable and threatened in any way, then make them aware that is **okay to be rude**. They don't need to be polite to strangers. They need to understand that their safety comes first, so get away as quickly as possible and find help.

Life Lesson: *Street Smart people recognize danger and become vigilant when fleeing to safety. It is not the time to be polite; strangers have not earned your trust and respect.*

We need to help the child first understand and recognize clues that they maybe entering into a dangerous situation. Any person that the child does not know is considered to be a stranger. Being street smart means that I will avoid strangers at all cost. If approached by a stranger and you feel uncomfortable in any way, then simply run to safety as quickly as possible. Taking action is your choice and now is the time to get away immediately.

A street smart person understands the importance of not engaging in a conversation with a stranger or any person who makes them feel uncomfortable. The bad person is trying to trick you into a harmful situation. As a child, if you answer any questions posed by these people, you maybe falling right into the trap.

These people who pose harm to our children are playing a game as they try to learn more about you. When the child does engage in a conversation, they begin to share personal information without realizing how damaging it can be. A child may tell these people that their parents are at work and they are home alone for a couple of hours after school. The child may say he or she is an only child and the parents are divorced. This information is exactly what a bad person is looking for so that they can take advantage of and possibly harm a child.

These people who mean harm to our children are clever and may offer you a gift or say your parents asked them to pick you up. Be street smart and don't listen or engage in the conversation and run as fast as you can away from this encounter. It is important for our children to understand that their body language is also a form of communication.

If a child is walking around alone with his head down and shoulders slumped over, it is a sign of insecurity and low self-esteem. This is the ideal victim for the bad guy because they want to dominate and take advantage of you.

I teach my boys to walk around with their heads up, chest out, shoulders back and make eye contact with everyone like they own the world. This is someone who is street smart and their body language represents **confidence and strength**. The bad people out there do not want to deal with this type of child because they will be more difficult to manipulate and take advantage of.

Street Smart children should always check with a parent or trusted adult before going anywhere, accepting anything, or getting into a car with anyone. Children should try to stay in groups when they are going outside or traveling someplace like a shopping mall. Safety in numbers is a good way to prevent bad people from even attempting to approach our kids.

Children also need to understand that their body belongs to them and they have a right to say no if anybody tries to touch them or treat them in a way that makes them feel uncomfortable. A street smart kid will tell his parents or trusted adult right away if he or she has ever encountered such a terrible ordeal.

Life Lesson: *Trust your instincts and watch for clues that you may be in danger. Once detected then don't hesitate become vigilant as you flee to safety.*

Open communication between parent and child is important to help resolve situations that may occur with your child. The child needs to understand that they can come to you with anything, whether it is a simple problem or something out of the ordinary.

Today, with all the new technology, including the Internet, chat rooms, Myspace, Face Book, cell phone, texting, twitter, etc., it is crucial that children and adults refrain from giving out personal information. **Online predators** pretend to be your age in chat rooms. They are trying to trick you and tempt you into meeting with them. My two children are not allowed to visit chat rooms because it is too dangerous and we monitor their face book page. Kids today are sexting, which is dangerous and illegal.

Sexting is when a person will transmit sexually explicit messages or videos via a cell phone. Sexting cases are not only dangerous for children because they are engaging in a dangerous behavior but it is illegal. This is a federal offense with both the sender and receiver of this type of communication being charged with child pornography. These sexual images may also be sent to several friends and before you know it the whole town has a copy and if you thought gossip was hurtful. We all need to be **street smart** here and educate our kids not to engage in this "sexting" type of behavior. Parents need to check your kid's profiles that they may have created with any of these new networking sites and be aware that your child may have set up two profiles one for their friends and the other usually more innocent for the family.

Lenny Silva

I have been educating my two sons not to engage in another new and terrible trend, which is called "Cyber Bullying". This is a practice when teens will taunt and make fun of each other with instant messages, e-mails, texting, and face-book postings. Some kids will group together and pick on or bully another child. The horrible things that kids will say to each other is frustrating to parents and if your child is a victim of this they need to know that you are here to support and love them. I ask my two sons to be **street smart** and not to pay attention or engage in any of this bad behavior. Some kids cannot handle this bullying and are committing suicide at a very young age. We all need to be vigilant to prevent and stop "Cyber Bullying" and keeping all the children safe.

Adults are now having problems with identity theft. They also need to become more street smart and avoid disclosing personal information such as names, date of birth and social security numbers over the telephone and on the Internet. Bad people are running scams claiming to be employees at your bank or government officials updating their records and ask you for all your personal information. A street smart person would recognize this as a threat and hang up the phone.

As an employee of a bank, I can tell you firsthand that we never call customers asking for personal information. If you are a customer, then we already have your information. Each company you may deal with all have the same privacy and confidentiality policies. They will not call you asking for this information. It is a trap to get your personal information, so you must be rude and just hang up the telephone.

As adults, remember it is okay for you to be rude when dealing with these people on the telephone. We can be polite and keep our manners ready for people whom we meet face to face and trust. We are all too nice and that opens the door for bad people to take advantage of us. This is most prevalent in the elderly population and children.

Adults and children should not engage in conversations with these scam artists over the telephone because they will trick you by trying to get your personal information and you are at risk for bodily harm or identity theft.

Women who may live alone, the elderly and children of all ages are all at risk if they disclose too much information to people they first meet on the Internet or other new communication devices available. Remember the words **street smart** and begin to condition your mind by making it stronger as you become more focused. Hang up the telephone when asked for your personal information.

There are so many bad people out there lurking in Internet chat rooms who are targeting both children and adults. The new technology is great, but also has a downside because so many bad people out there use it to gain financial success and commit acts of violence against others. We trust the wrong people and in the end we get hurt. Our children must learn to recognize these potentially dangerous situations and simply avoid them all together.

Life Lesson: *Don't disclose any personal information over the phone or Internet.*

There are many people in this world who are brilliant in the classroom and are earning doctorate degrees from the most prestigious colleges. You may come across some of these same people in your classroom. These same people also may lack common sense and are not street smart.

In the game of basketball you are allowed ten seconds to get the ball over half court and if not, you turn the ball over to the other team. I like this ten-second rule and in life began using it to teach my two sons about safety. It became a street smart lesson called **the ten-second rule.**

Many people get hurt while on vacation and it could easily be avoided if they would only stop and take ten seconds and think before acting. I visited the beautiful islands located through out the Caribbean. Most tourists love to rent mopeds and ride around the islands going sightseeing.

The last time I was visiting such an island, my wife and I decided we would do just that and rent mopeds. I mentioned this to a police officer client of mine. The police officer offered me some free advice. He asked me when was the last time I rode a moped. I said never. He said "If you have never ridden a moped then why would you put your life at risk and rent one here on the island?" I said that was a good point. He also went on to say that most of the tourists who rent mopeds get hurt and some get killed. The local drivers do not yield for these types of vehicles and when an accident occurs the car wins and the moped loses. The police officer was giving me a street smart lesson and he was 100% correct.

Whenever I travel on vacation now, I take ten seconds to think about any activity we decide to try. I consider my experience and safety performing that activity. You may decide that it is not worth the risk of injury and go onto another activity.

We all get a false sense of security while on vacation thinking nothing bad will happen to us. That is the exact point we stop thinking, get caught up with the beautiful surroundings and want to let loose and enjoy the adventure. You can still have fun but be street smart and take ten seconds to think things through. If you are still uncomfortable, then just pass on that activity and find something else to do. We all need to get away and relax, but at the end of the day it is not worth it if you get seriously hurt or killed.

I am not trying to scare you or ruin your vacation. I want you to come home safely and remind you that you are away from home and sometimes in a foreign country. Take ten seconds to think before you act and maybe it will prevent you from getting hurt. Be careful when you venture away from the resort that you maybe staying at.

Life Lesson: *Think before you act, especially when away from home.*

A few years back there was a very unfortunate incident that happened on an island. A lovely young woman disappeared while visiting that island with her high school senior class. It was all over the news and I am sure you all heard about it and know her name.

This beautiful young girl went out on the town one night with her girlfriends. They had some alcoholic beverages and apparently this young lady left the bar alone with three men. She was never found again and my heart goes out to her and her family. I am sick about this story and as a parent cannot imagine all the pain and suffering they have had to endure.

Let us all become street smart and understand the **code of friendship** when you are going out for some fun with your friends. *"This same group of friends that goes out together comes home together"*. It is that simple and there are no exceptions. You all need to make a contract, stick to the plan and look out for one another. If someone in your group meets another person they like at a party or nightclub, exchanging numbers and making arrangements to meet the next day or night is the safe and smart thing to do. If you are drunk your judgment is impaired and you are not thinking straight.

The other friends in your group need to step in and help you make the right decision or the whole group needs to take control of the situation. Remember your safety is first and foremost above everything else. You can explain to the person that you first met that all of you came as a group and you all will be leaving as a group. There will be no compromising. This is a **safety rule** and you are just being street smart.

If your group has a plan before heading out, then stick to it. Enjoy yourselves and have fun but your parents would like you to come home safely and I am sure you would like that too. Remember safety comes first and your group all need to agree on this and be there for each other. Tomorrow always comes and we all want you around to see it.

I think that this incident on that island for that missing girl could have been easily avoided. **In my opinion**, I put a lot of the blame on the friends who allowed this girl to leave the bar with three strange men. The friends of this young girl broke a common rule in friendship and somebody paid for it with their life. If you all came together, you should all leave together. The friends should have stepped up and taken control of this situation and not allowed the girl to leave alone with three men.

Life Lesson: *All for one and one for all. Have fun but take ten seconds and think.*

Let us all learn from this terrible tragedy and remember to be **street smart** and take care of each other. If the people you meet give you a hard time, notify the bouncer at the club or the police. They are there to help and try to make your night enjoyable, especially when you are a tourist in a foreign country.

Traveling abroad is exciting but can also be very dangerous. You may be in a foreign country and not be familiar with the language and culture. A movie came out a while ago and it was about a retired CIA agent who was the perfect **street smart** father. He was well trained and could defend himself in any situation and was always prepared.

His sixteen-year old daughter wanted to travel abroad with her sixteen-year old friend. She lied to her father about having parental supervision at the place where they were staying. The two young pretty girls were leaving the airport in this foreign country and were hailing a cab to the place where they were staying. The girls were approached by a stranger and after only a couple of minutes began to share personal information that would become very damaging to their safety. They allowed the stranger to share a cab with them as he followed them right to the doorstep of their apartment.

They told this guy that they were staying alone and what floor they were on. This stranger was the lookout and information gathering bad guy. He would then contact his other scumbag friends. Within minutes and without the chance to even unpack their luggage or go to the bathroom, several men had broken into the apartment and kidnapped the girls. These two girls were taken within a half hour after landing in this foreign country.

This is a horrible story and the tragedy could have been avoided if they were street smart and remembered the golden rule to never share personal information with strangers. They should have been rude and not engaged in conversations with a strange man at the airport. They should have declined sharing a cab ride and could have lied to the man and said their father was waiting for them. Make up anything to get out of a dangerous situation.

This storyline came from a movie, but in real life it is unfortunate that these types of situations occur quite frequently. Young girls are being kidnapped and then forced into prostitution and never seen again. **Street smart** people always have an exit plan and are leery when meeting people for the first time. We are so trusting that we sometimes do not stop and think for **ten seconds** about the possibility of something going wrong.

Once you begin to share personal information with strangers, especially in foreign countries, you are only getting yourself into potential trouble. You are increasing the odds that you will become a victim of a violent act. A street smart person avoids these types of situations and if approached by a stranger then recognize the clues and be prepared to defend yourself by getting away from it and be vigilant in your efforts.

Life Lesson: *Don't be so trusting with people you meet for the first time. Trust is earned.*

If a bad situation happens then try to remain calm keeping a cool head and start looking for options to get to safety. We all make mistakes, but the **street smart** person will become creative and vigilant in their efforts to get away. We do not have to be in a foreign country to get into trouble. We can get ourselves into plenty of trouble right here at home.

I have a friend who had a bad experience at a party while he was in college. They were at a keg party and somebody played a joke and slipped something into his cup while he was not looking. Well, a practical joke nearly turned deadly. The boy had an allergic reaction and had to be rushed to the hospital from the combination of the drug and the alcohol.

A **Street smart party person** will always remember to keep an eye on his drink at all times. This can be a soda or an alcoholic beverage. I would only drink from a can or bottle and open the container myself. If I did not hear the can open or the bottle cap twist off then I always felt that it may have been tampered with and threw it out. I would then go get myself a new drink and make sure that I opened it. *If, I had to go to the bathroom I would take the drink with me.* I would never leave it behind. If a friend opened a drink for me, well, I would take it with me and pour it down the toilet. I would then go get myself a new drink and open it myself. I know it sounds a little bit paranoid but trust nobody with your drinks, especially at a keg party.

A street smart person trusts nobody. Like with my friend from college, a joke can have a bad outcome. In the end, the person who thought he was playing a joke and the person who was on the receiving end of the joke both ended up with bad outcomes. **Your safety comes first.** Have fun but be street smart and take ten seconds to think before you act. The two are no longer friends and sometimes a joke can have serious consequences.

The times you spend in high school and college should be the best times of your life. You have no life pressures like paying a mortgage or working full time to support your family. As your parents, we want you to enjoy life. When kids go off to college and leave home for the first time, they want to experience everything within the first weekend. They go to their first keg party and get so drunk that some kids actually die from alcohol poisoning.

Street smart people understand that **everything in moderation** is the best way to live your life. They also understand that you do not have to follow the crowd. Be a leader and just say no or be creative and get yourself out of the situation. You could always say you have a bad stomach and medically cannot consume much alcohol.

It is okay for you to be creative to get yourself out of a tough situation. I had a friend who would always crack open a new beer along with all the rest of us but would then take the bottle into the bathroom and pour out ninety percent of it. We always thought that he was drinking just as many beers as the rest of us, but the next morning he was always the first person up and off for a morning jog. He was street smart and we were stupid as we dealt with our hang over the next day.

Life Lesson: *Be a leader and not a follower; avoid excessive alcohol consumption.*

He was a **street smart** person because he still enjoyed having fun with us, but poured out ninety percent of the beer he opened and never had to deal with a hangover the next day. As parents, we want you all to have experiences and adventures. It just seems that today some kids do not get a second chance and terrible things happen. **I want you all to just think for 10 seconds and try to avoid them.**

If you are going to go to that next keg party, have a plan and be prepared. You may be facing **peer pressure** to drink in excess. Be prepared because there are ways for you to still have fun and learn how to not engage in that excessive behavior.

You can always visit the bathroom and pour half the beer out. You are in college now so use your brain and prepare yourself before you get to the party. A street smart person will never drive drunk and never get into a car with anyone who is drunk.

I always tell my two sons to call me any time of night and I will come and get them and drive everyone else home. I will not be mad and I will be happy to drive the kids home safely. I actually enjoy doing this because then I get a chance to listen to all the stories and experiences that they may have encountered at the party.

Life Lesson: *Make a contract with your child to not drive drunk or get in any car with somebody else who is drunk. Create a cab ride home envelope and leave fifty dollars in it and tell your children to take the cash before they leave the house if they are going off to a party. If they drink then leave the car at the party and use the cash for a cab ride home. They can replace the money at another time and remind them that the money is for a cab ride and not a handout for every night they go out for other events.*

I have an attorney friend who was telling me a story. He knew a young man about fifteen years old who got called down to the principal's office. This kid was attending private school at the time. The principal and a local police officer were in the office and they wanted to get some information from this student about some trouble that had occurred on school property the day before.

The student was under the age of eighteen, so technically the police officer and school principal could not demand that he answer questions without the presence of a parent, legal guardian, or lawyer. If a child volunteers to offer information and answer questions, then they are on their own and what you say can and will be used against you.

That is exactly the mistake this child made when he admitted to being at the scene of this incident but had nothing to do with the vandalism. He did not want to name the other child, who was a friend, and the person who actually committed all the vandalism. This child chose to answer questions without his parents being present during the interrogation. He was not street smart and decided to answer some tough questions.

The principal and police officer threw the book at this boy and expelled him from school because he admitted to being at the scene. The boy who actually committed the act of vandalism got away with it because they had no proof. This child was told that he did not have to answer questions until his parents arrived. If he had only waited ten more minutes his parents would have probably helped him to answer the questions better and he would have avoided being expelled from school.

Life Lesson *God gave you two ears and one mouth for a reason. You learn more when you listen than when you do all the talking. Take the advice* *and always wait for your parents when any adult with authority wants to conduct an interrogation.*

It is important to understand your rights. If you are ever under arrest or are asked to visit the principal's office then understand your rights before you speak. If you are under the age of eighteen then simply ask to have your parent or legal guardian present before you answer any questions. It does not mean that you are guilty of anything by asking for this.

You must understand that when you are being interrogated **fear will set in.** You may not understand the question correctly and then you will offer the wrong information. The people who are interrogating you are wise and form questions in a way that make you feel comfortable to answer. It can be a very intimidating process and confusing to you.

They may tell you that they are here to help you and do not want to see you get in trouble. It is a trap because in the end they are looking for you to confess and admit to something that you may not have done. **Street smart** people will listen and then remember that they have legal rights. Understanding these rights, they will just wait for help to arrive. I want everyone to understand that as a child, you have a right **not to answer** any questions from a person of authority without your parents present. Don't let them make you feel guilty or think that you are hiding something. You are being street smart by waiting for your parents. I would ask for a book to read until your parents or legal guardian arrive.

The child who was a witness to an act of vandalism at his school was also a victim in this situation. He was expelled from school for admitting that he was at the scene of the crime but he had nothing to do with the actual crime. The school wanted to send a message to everyone else and the wrong boy paid the ultimate price.

If your children would take ten seconds to think before acting then maybe it would help keep them safe and out of trouble. If your children would take ten seconds to always have an exit plan for getting out of any building that you enter then you will be better prepared to flee to safety in the event of an emergency.

Many years ago in the news there was a horrible shooting at Columbine High School. Two students lost their will to live and respect for human life. They went on a shooting rampage and killed their teachers and classmates. It was a tragic event.

When you walk into a building take ten seconds to look around and know how you can get out in the event of an emergency. If you are going into the same building daily, like your school, then you should have a pretty good idea where all the exits are.

Your school is supposed to be a place of learning and a chance for you to make new friends, play sports and have fun. Today that has changed. Now we all need to be street smart and understand that another school tragedy could occur and you need to be prepared. I hope you never have to face what those kids had to deal with at Columbine. We know it can happen again but we are not sure where or when.

Life Lesson: *Become familiar with all exits when entering any building. Know how to get out safely from any building that you enter.*

Every day that you go to school, I want you to look around and be aware of all exits including windows. Check the doorknobs in your classrooms and see if they have locks. If you hear noise that sounds like a firecracker, hopefully that is all it is. If you are starting to get that gut feeling again, this is your survival instinct telling you it is time to get street smart and start looking for the exits or for places to hide.

If you hear about any person, even someone you consider a friend, who indicates that they have a weapon and make threats that they will use it against a teacher or another student, you must report this immediately. Notify a parent or someone you trust. Unfortunately, these things happen in society today. We do get warning signals and with swift action the situation maybe avoided and lives saved.

I have been telling you all along that if you become just a little street smart and prepare for the unexpected, you will survive a tragedy more often than someone who is not prepared. Street smart people are mentally tougher than others. They are prepared, keep cool heads and react to the situation by taking action and fleeing to safety.

When a bad situation begins, you will become scared just like everyone else but you are street smart. You understand your exit plan and know how to get out of any place that you have entered because you took the time to prepare. Remember, it is too late for preparation once a bad situation begins. Now is the time to react so that you can look for options to flee to safety. You always want to be vigilant in your efforts while trying to get out of a bad situation. When entering a building, take ten seconds to plan an exit strategy.

Life Lesson: *Trust your gut instincts and err on the side of caution.*

I do not want to scare anyone but I am only trying to get you to think and understand the importance of a little preparation. I started my journey as a street smart person in Little League. After my coach taught me the **skill** about being prepared to make a play prior to the ball being hit my way, I applied that in my life.

Life Lesson: *We can learn much from athletics and apply them to our everyday lives.*

I took a skill I learned from the game of baseball and it was an awakening for me. I began to apply that skill to my life and would try to be a little prepared in everything that I did. I had a lot of fun growing up and always felt like nothing bad would ever happen to me. I made my own luck by avoiding dangerous situations but also made some mistakes as a young adult, I was far from perfect but lucky to survive my mistakes.

Today, as an employee of a bank, I am required to be aware of any people loitering around the branch prior to it opening up for business. These people might look suspicious and out of place. I need to trust my instincts and if things do not feel right, then I have been trained to get back in my car and drive away.

Life Lesson: *I wish you all to be street smart and better prepared for life and the unexpected events that may thrust you into danger.*

This chapter was designed to help you be aware and become a little street smart. Maybe your preparation will help you or a friend get out of a tough spot. As a father, I want you to have fun but come home safely so you can live to enjoy another day. I want all parents to understand the importance to help keep your kids safe. You can help your child by not allowing them to have their cell phones or computers in their bedroom at night.

A parent should also have all passwords for any network site such as facebook and myspace. There are also many different types of software available so that as a parent we can hook up to our child's cell phone or computer to closely monitor every digital step your child may take. **Communication** with your child is crucial explaining to them that you respect their privacy but until they turn eighteen they must fully understand all the risk and potential dangers that can occur when they use the new technology that is available to them. You own the house, cell phone and computer so set the rules. I truly believe that as a parent we need to stay close to our children until they turn twenty-five years old. They will become an adult at the age of eighteen but I feel that they still need our guidance with regards to their finances, safety, until they turn twenty-five years old. They maybe living out on there own, married, and bad things can happen in an instant but stay in touch.

Life Lesson: *You're never too old to still listen and learn from fatherly advice. Identity theft victims are being targeted at all ages and young adults under the age of twenty-five are most vulnerable.*

If you would like more information with regards to identity theft including prevention and reporting then check out the United States Department Of Justice web site at WWW.USDOJ.gov. Once you're at the home page you can scroll down to the right and **click on report a crime**. You then scroll down to the left and under the category of computer and Internet crime **click on identity theft and crime for more information**. It is important to notify the credit reporting agencies immediately and you will find the phone numbers and instructions for these agencies on this same page.

If you would like to learn more about ways to help keep your kids safe while using all the new technology devices that are available to them then check out another informational website by the Bristol County Sheriffs Offices at WWW.BSCO-MA.us

Once you are on the home page **click under public programs** and then **click public education**. Then you can **click on parental resources and links**, which will list several other sites all about ways to help keep your kid's safe and educating them on all the benefits and pitfalls while using these new technology devices.

Life Lesson: *Parents must be vigilant when it comes to keeping your underage child safe and teach them to be a little **street smart**. Knowledge is power.*

Second Inning

Dream Car By Len Zen

While playing baseball in college, my coach would tell us about the importance of staying positive. We had a big game scheduled in a couple of days against an opponent, who on paper, looked so much better than us. Our coach would ask us to forget about their record and remain positive and focus on what we could control and how we play.

I played my worst baseball game against this team. I was really embarrassed about the mistakes I had made, which helped our team to lose. I was not looking forward to playing this team again and starting thinking about the possibility of repeating such a horrible performance. To make matters worse, we were hosting this game at our home field and I would have a lot of family and friends coming to watch my team and me play.

This was a very big game because we needed to win so that our team would qualify for the NCAA tournament. The opposing team also needed to win so they could also qualify for the same tournament. It all came down to this one game and the winner would advance and the loser would go home for the season.

Our team and I both wanted this tournament bid so badly. It would have been our first selections in the NCAA tournament for our team in a very long time. Every team wanted to get into this tournament. It is the elite tournament throughout the country and we had a chance to become a national champion.

I was dealing with a lot of pressure and finding it hard to sleep, as the game was only a couple of days away. I remember the coach telling me not to live in the past and not to dwell on past mistakes. I could not get mentally stronger and snap out of the negative feelings that seem to be consuming me.

I was irritable and not very nice to my parents and friends. I was not acting like my jovial self and thinking about this big game started making me feel like I was going crazy. I had so many negative thoughts going through my head. I kept thinking about all the bad plays and errors that I had made in the last meeting with this opponent.

I really felt like it was my fault that we lost that first game against this team. My teammates reminded me that they played badly as well, and in baseball we win and lose as a team. They tried to lift my spirits but I kept feeling sorry for myself. I appreciated the team support, but thought it may be best for the team if I sat this game out. It was the first time that I did not want to play. I was so down on myself and negative about my last performance against this team. I just could not forget about the past.

Life Lesson: *If, self-doubt crowds your mind, forget it and remain positive. Self-doubt only allows fear to set in and this leads to failure.*

At my next baseball practice, I approached my coach and told him all about my negative thoughts and lack of confidence. I said maybe it would be best if he started somebody else at shortstop so our team had a better chance of winning. My coach reminded me about all the great games that I played this season and all my clutch late inning hits. He indicated that we had our best chance of winning only if I was in the starting line up. He was a great motivator and helpful to all the players.

He would remind me not to dwell on the mistakes that I made in the past because I could not change it or control what had already happened. We must forget about the past, focus on today and how we can improve with a positive attitude. Focus on winning the game.

My coach taught us about being able to focus on those things that you can control and forget about all those things that you cannot control. In the game of baseball, as a player, I can always practice harder and work on improving my skills to become a more complete player. We as players cannot control the bad calls an umpire may make or the success the other team may have had on us in the past. My coach would always ask us to visualize our team performing well and winning.

There is so much we all can learn from having a positive attitude and having the ability to learn from past mistakes. Use that knowledge to help you improve your game and your team's success. It is easy to say but how do we become mentally stronger and actually make it happen? How do we put our past behind us and move on?

I appreciated my coach for his kind words and starting feeling a little bit better. I honestly still had some doubt about this next big game and my abilities to help my team win. We all have been there, feeling like we made mistakes and not sure how we can learn from them or make the situation better.

It was time for me to try and move on from that game and just let it go. The past is the past and I could not turn back the clock and replay that game. I played badly and made mistakes. I needed to move forward, learn from my mistakes and not repeat them.

It all sounded good, but like most people who are competitive in athletics, you hold yourself to a higher standard. You know that you can play better and you always want to have a great game every time. I needed to focus on the next game. This was something that I could control. I needed to forget about the last game that was over two weeks ago and therefore out of my control.

Life Lesson: *If, you feel like your situation is beyond your control, pray and have faith. Focus on what you can control and let go of what you can't. There is always a tomorrow.*

The next day I was leaving my house and was driving to baseball practice. I drove a beat up old car and still remember all the fun times I had with my first car. It may not have looked the best, but it certainly helped get me to and from school every day and got me to all my baseball games without breaking down.

It was a very reliable car and it may not have been my dream car but it was all that I could afford at the time. We all like to dream, and for me the ideal dream car was a *Chevrolet Corvette Convertible*. This car was triple black, which has a black convertible top, black leather interior and black exterior.

To me, this was the ultimate driving machine. Even though I never test drove one, it appealed to me. One day I wanted to own a car like this. What I love most about dreaming of a car like this or winning the lottery, is the peace of mind and instant gratification you get mentally from that image of actually being that lucky.

I found myself beginning to start thinking more positively. I felt that I could accomplish anything while having these mid afternoon dreaming sessions. I believe this was the first time I understood what visualization techniques were all about. It is a process for us to change the way we think. If you are feeling negative, visualize something to help you snap out of that state of mind and become more positive.

It felt as if I was actually tricking myself into believing that I was driving my dream car and not this beat up old clunker. I noticed that my mood had changed and I was feeling much better about everything, including going to class and playing in this next big baseball game. I started to realize that it is only a game so try and have fun. I needed to trust my skills and abilities.

While I was driving my beat up old car and dreaming of my luxury car of choice, I had a thought. I started to think about my coach telling us about using visualization techniques to help keep us positive. In any car, whether it is your dream car or broken down clunker, they all have a **rear view mirror** and a **front windshield**.

On that day while I was driving to school and looking out my front windshield, I had a breakthrough. I decided right then and there that the **front windshield** could represent all the opportunities that lie before me. I began to feel more positive knowing that just by looking forward, I could possibly change some outcomes and achieve success, not failure.

I had more control over those goals that I had set for today and tomorrow. I could work harder in the classroom and on the baseball field by improving my skills. I began to believe that looking out that front windshield offered a positive solution and my negative thoughts began to fade away. My future seemed a little brighter. I was now gaining mental strength for this upcoming big game.

Life Lesson: *When you want to complain, identify a solution instead and succeed.*

The **rear view mirror** in my car represented my yesterdays and past experiences. I could chose to live my life and dwell on the past by looking in the rear view mirror, or I could become mentally stronger and focus on all the good things that may occur while being positive and looking out the front windshield. Learn from your mistakes that are located in the rear view mirror, but move on and focus on the positive outcomes that can happen for you while looking out the front windshield.

Life lesson: *Whenever you are thinking about the past or worrying about the future, instead focus your energy on the present. The here and now is where your power is the greatest. Try to block out all those things that you can't control and focus on those that you can.*

These two objects that we use everyday while driving became symbols in helping me to decide on how I want to live and tackle everyday life experiences and challenges. They would help me to snap out of my current state of mind and turn any negative situation into something positive.

I started to laugh as it became so clear to me that my whole outlook and attitude had also changed. I started looking out the front windshield and realized the opportunity I had to prove to myself, coach, teammates and the other opponent how good I could be in that next game.

I started to think about how I could use my speed to help score runs for my team. I began to process in my mind all the skills, abilities, and strengths that I had as a player. These skills if used properly would help our team succeed and improve our chance to win the big game. I starting feeling great and when I got to school I could not wait to tell my teammates and coach about my breakthrough. We had a team meeting prior to practice that afternoon. Our coach wanted to go over our assignments for the big game.

The coach handed out the pitching assignments and explained that this was our last game of the regular season so he wanted to use both our top pitchers for this big game. He would start our number one guy and have him go three innings and then come back with our number two guy for the next three innings. He would then have our two best closers come in and hopefully shut them down for the rest of the game.

He then went to all our position players and indicated who will be starting and where they would be placed in the batting lineup. He wanted me at shortstop and leading off which is where I had been during the whole season. The coach had a great team speech and really pushed hard on all of us to forget about our last encounter with this team.

Life Lesson: *Whenever you face critics, remember to be positive and focus only on being the best that you can be. You must believe in order to achieve.*

The coach went around the room and looked at each player on the team and asked for any feedback. He wanted to know how we were feeling about this big task that lie ahead of us. We had a great relationship with our coach and he liked that we were always very honest with him.

All the players liked his game plan, especially the pitching rotation. Some of our players were still feeling the effects of our last outing with this team. They were having all those negative thoughts and were still dwelling on the past just like I had been for the past few days. If I did not have my mental breakthrough in the car earlier that day, I probably would have been right there with them.

Unintentionally, my teammates came across as having negative attitudes. It was just the way things sounded. They were all great ballplayers and teammates, but they sounded just like me when I was talking with the coach the other day.

I stood up in the meeting and told everyone about my revelation and dream car visualization. I explained about how the rearview mirror represented our past experiences and the front windshield represented the future, with all the opportunities that lie ahead for us. I was so positive and confident in my speech. I reminded all the players that each of them brought so many positive and strong skills as baseball players. We needed to band together, look out that front windshield, move forward to success and destroy that team. We needed to remember that team was standing in our way of achieving our goal to make it to the NCAA tournament.

I told them that I did not want to think about the last game anymore. It was over with and was located in my rear view mirror. I don't live life anymore by looking into my rear view mirror. At the end of the day it is out of my control because these things have already happened. Nothing positive can come from looking back at those reflections. We cannot turn back the clock so we need to move on as a team.

I told my teammates that I had been miserable lately. I had been having difficulty sleeping, eating and I was treating everyone around me badly because I was living my life dwelling in the past. I did not want to be miserable anymore and living in the past was a waste of my time and energy. I told them that after I started looking out my front windshield and envisioned all the great opportunities that lie ahead for me, and our team, my whole outlook and attitude changed for the better. I felt more positive energy and began to look forward to this big challenge.

Life lesson: *Whenever you face those naysayers, remember the people who believed in you. Have confidence in yourself remain positive and you will succeed.*

My coach was very pleased that somehow I was able to get mentally stronger. I used the new dream car technique to not only help myself, but also help my teammates prepare for the big game. He told me after the meeting that I had become a better leader by sharing with the team a way to become more positive.

We were all feeling much better and looking forward to having a great practice. As I stepped onto the baseball field that afternoon between those white chalked foul lines, I imagined myself actually stepping into my dream car. I felt like I was actually driving the Corvette convertible.

I felt so great pretending to be sitting in my dream car, racing down the highway with the music cranking and the wind blowing through my hair. In my mind, it was such a great place to be. I had never felt such positive energy before and my confidence level was so high. I could accomplish anything on the ball field. Everything was within my reach.

Life Lesson: *If you feel like you can't do it, know that you can do all things through Him who gives you strength. Trust yourself and your skills; have faith and you will succeed.*

I became so relaxed and focused while I was taking my one hundred ground balls during infield practice. We had an assistant coach that would hit me at least that many ground balls every practice. I loved it and never got tired. I would wear out that poor coach because he did get tired of hitting so many baseballs. He was a great assistant coach who took his time hitting not only to me but also to my teammates. He hit ground balls and fly balls every day at practice. It was a great practice for everyone. We all seemed to be more focused and nobody was goofing off. Our head coach did not have to make anyone run for misbehaving.

I think my teammates were also stepping into their dream cars. We all were very confident and positive when we went onto the field, by practicing hard and getting ready for the big game. Everybody seemed to have this new swagger and it was quite remarkable to notice this transformation in everybody's attitude.

The big day finally arrived for us to play this team that had beat down on us previously by ten runs. I left my house a little earlier than usual that day and sat in my driveway for a few extra minutes. I took a look in my rearview mirror and for a brief moment starting thinking about the last game and my mistakes. I quickly changed and looked out that front windshield, big crack and all. I went over in my mind all the positive things I could accomplish today in this big game. I kept telling myself we would win this game today. No matter how the game starts off, stay positive. If I make a mistake, forget about it and move on and win.

Life lesson: *When you fail, find the lesson in it and then recall a time when you have succeeded. Record every positive outcome today and use them in the future.*

I arrived at school and got dressed. The whole team walked out to the ball field and took our pre-game warm ups. We were all feeling very confident but we were much quieter than usual. I could see on everyone's face that they were ready and I was feeling nervous.

Finally, the big game began. As I took the field and jumped over the third base foul line, I pretended once again that I was jumping right into my dream car. All of a sudden those nervous feelings went away. I became so focused and my thoughts were so clear. When you hear people say that someone is in the zone, well that is exactly where my mind was that day.

I was having a career day in the field and at the plate. I was playing a perfect game and making no mistakes. My team was also playing unbelievably well and our two starting pitchers accomplished their goals just the way coach had mapped out. They both finished strong, but after nine innings we were losing 3 to 1 and we had our last at bats.

In the bottom of the ninth inning our sixth, seventh, eight, and ninth batters were up first. In order for me to get a chance to bat, these players needed to get on base any way they could. We needed two runs to tie and three to win the most important game of our lives and get into the NCAA tournament.

We were off to a bad start in the ninth inning as our first two batters struck out and we were quickly down two outs. The pressure was mounting and the outlook was bleak for us to pull off this victory. Then our eighth hitter lined a base hit up the middle and we suddenly had one runner on base.

Our next hitter was quickly down two strikes and no balls, when he fouled off three tough pitches. He worked the pitcher, putting on a good battle, and the count was now three balls and two strikes. The next pitch was low and he managed to walk, putting our runners on first and second base. The game tying run was now on first base but there were two outs.

The stage was now set for yours truly, our lead off hitter me. We had two outs, it was the bottom of the ninth inning with two base runners on, and at the time our team was losing three to one. The other manager had seen enough. His starting pitcher threw well that day, but obviously was getting tired. The manager made a pitching change and went to his closer. He was a big right-handed pitcher, about six feet five inches tall and threw gas. He had a side arm delivery where he drops down and drives his body towards the right-handed batter as he delivers the pitch. I was a right-handed batter and watching him warm up noticed he hid the ball well and knew it would be a difficult at bat for me.

The place was packed with family and friends and our season finale now ended up in my hands. I felt alone out there in the batter's box. It was just the pitcher and I. I would get myself mentally prepared with anger towards the opposing pitcher because we were heading into a one on one battle. For a brief moment, I did experience some doubt and knew that was not good because any doubt before heading into the batters box only leads to failure. You can never allow fear or doubt to set in your mind or you will fail.

Life lesson: *If, you feel alone, think of all the people who have helped to prepare you along the way gaining strength and confidence as you face any challenge.*

I began to get very nervous thinking about all the things that could go wrong. I imagined standing at the plate watching three pitches go by and striking out, thus ending our season. I also started thinking about our last game once again against this team and how badly I performed at the plate that day. I faced this pitcher that day and he struck me out.

I had been feeling great all day and was having a really good game, but could not focus or get myself back on track. I needed something to help me snap out of all this negative thinking. I knew that I needed to snap out of it because thinking negative thoughts while trying to hit a baseball only leads to disaster. I needed to get mentally strong or I was doomed to fail.

The parking lot was located behind the baseball field and you could easily watch cars coming and going. This is where most of the faculty who taught at the college parked. What do I see but a professor parking his car? He was getting out of a black corvette convertible. I was amazed and instantly thought he was driving my dream car. I know it sounds silly but after all that I had been through, the dream car visualization had helped me relax and concentrate on the game. I had been feeling negative again briefly and then I saw that car and laughed inside. I thought this must be a sign from God.

I was instructed by the home plate umpire to get into the batter's box because the pitcher had finished with his warm up throws. As I stepped into the batter's box, I imagined myself stepping right into my dream car and it was the one the college professor was driving. In your mind it is okay to borrow someone else's car. In reality, it is not a good idea to actually do it that would be stealing.

I had never felt so relaxed in my life. I was immediately back in the zone and focused on trying to beat the pitcher and make something good happen for my team. I was looking out that front windshield and had no time to even look in the rear view mirror. I was ready to take this challenge and give this pitcher the fight of his life. I was angry and confident as I took my place in the batters box. It was he or I and my team needed me.

The home crowd was going crazy. They were so loud cheering my teammates and me on. As I entered into the batter's box, for some reason I had blocked out all the noise and it was silence in my mind. It felt as if the pitcher and I were the only people around.

I was so focused looking at the pitcher. He was the only thing that I saw and he delivered the first pitch and blew it right by me for strike one. I stepped out of the batter's box and took a practice swing and then got right back in there for another try. Here comes the second pitch and I swung as hard as I could but missed the ball completely as he changed speeds and threw me a change up for strike two. I looked so awful on these first two pitches and we were now down to our last strike.

I stepped out of the batter's box and began to talk to myself. I was evaluating the first two pitches he threw to me. The first pitch was a fastball right by me, and then the second pitch he threw was a change up to completely confuse me.

The pitcher was winning our one on one battle. He had successfully thrown two balls by me. I watched his body language, as he was very confident that he was winning the battle and going to win this game for his team. I had seen his first two pitches and learned a little bit in the process. I had actually picked up where his release point was coming from as he delivered those first two pitches. I got back in the batter's box and had a very good feeling that he would try to throw a curve ball, middle of the plate and away from me as a waste pitch and try to get me to chase.

Life Lesson: *Concentrate on the task at hand and block out all distractions.*

It is a good strategy for a pitcher to do this because if the batter does make contact with the baseball and try to pull the ball they usually will pop it up. The batter may also hit an easy ground ball to the third basemen. I moved my body up more in the batter's box and closer to the plate to help me cover more of the outside corner of the plate in the event the pitch was heading that way. Here comes the third pitch and I guessed correctly. It was a curve ball and it started out on the middle of the plate and as it began to curve outside I swung the bat and drove the baseball over the first basemen's head. The baseball took one hop off the fence and landed in the right field corner for a fair ball.

The runners on first and second base scored easily to tie the ball game. Using my blazing speed, I ended up with a stand up triple. The place went crazy. Everyone on my team was jumping up and down and all the fans were screaming. I was standing there on third base after having come up with the greatest clutch hit of my college career.

Life lesson: *If, you are tired and drained, remember to never give up. Finish strong in everything that you do digging deep with focus and determination to succeed.*

I felt like I was on top of the world and so happy to help my team tie this ball game up. I honestly did not think anyone on my team or all the fans at the ballpark thought that I could have hit the ball. I really looked so awful on the first two pitches. This pitcher could really throw well and seemed to have me on the ropes. He struck me out the last time we faced and I redeemed myself and helped my team this time around.

I had done it and actually never felt nervous as that third and final pitch came towards me. I was so focused and could see the laces on the ball as it was spinning towards the outside corner of the plate. I knew it was a curve ball and just drove my hands and the bat through the hitting zone, making great contact with the baseball.

The pitcher was so upset with what had just occurred, he went from being confident and cocky to distraught. He hung his head down as he walked around the pitcher's mound. He could not believe that I hit the ball and he just stopped and was staring at me. I played it cool and did not want to be cocky and show him up on the outside.

Life Lesson: *Once you feel all is impossible, know that all things are possible with God.*

I was so excited that I had beaten this pitcher during our one on one battle today. I wanted to show good sportsmanship and not make him feel any worse than he already did. I also had bigger plans. I wanted to score the winning run because the game was not over and the score was tied. We still needed one more run to win and advance to the NCAA tournament.

The other coach decided to leave this pitcher in the game because he really only made three pitches and was not tired. Mentally, I saw something else that would give me an edge and a chance to score that winning run. I watched this pitcher's body language and confidence completely shatter right in front of me. I could feel his confidence dwindle away and he had lost his composure. He was looking directly into the rear view mirror and could only think about what had just happened. He had forgotten that the game was tied and they still had a chance to win if he could get our next batter out.

Life lesson: *Once you head into battle, visualize success; believe in yourself and win.*

The second batter in our line up was now ready and standing in the batter's box looking to take a crack at this pitcher and win the game for us with a base hit. I was now taking a really big lead on third base as the pitcher was looking at me prior to delivering the next pitch. The pitcher was so focused on watching me that he threw the next ball one bounce in front of home plate as it scurried away from the catcher.

I had watched the flight of the ball as it left the pitcher's arm. I anticipated that it could not reach the plate and began running as fast as I could towards home plate. The ball hit the front of the plate and bounced off the catcher's mask and went to the left towards the on deck batters circle, which was not that far away from home plate.

It was now a race to home plate between me and the pitcher who had to cover and take the throw from the catcher. I got such a great jump running towards home plate and I actually beat the throw. I slid into home plate ahead of the throw from their catcher to their pitcher and scored the winning run for our team. We won and our team would advance to the NCAA tournament. It was a great comeback win for our team.

We had beaten this team and knocked them out of the tournament. We were all amazed that we could rally together and win. The odds were stacked against us but we stuck together and finished on top. Nobody believed that we had a chance to win. We were two runs down in the bottom of the ninth inning with two outs and two strikes on me. It was awesome!

Life lesson: *Anytime you face a setback, think of it as a defining moment that will lead to a future accomplishment. Learn from the setback, gain strength and move forward.*

That day, we were all acting like little kids enjoying our comeback victory. The home team crowd was so pleased. They all witnessed our team come together as a group and with determination we pulled off the greatest upset and played the best game of our season.

As I look back, I consider it one of the greatest days in my life. In the weeks leading up to that big game, I had been dealing with so many emotions. I had so much self-doubt and was unhappy with myself. I finally realized that dwelling on the past is no way to live.

For me, besides having my two children and celebrating my wedding day, this was truly the greatest day in my life. Against all odds, we won the game. It turned out to be a perfect game for me. I went five for five at the plate, making no errors in the field and that clutch hit triple driving in two runs tying the game with two strikes is something that I will never forget.

I have heard people talk about mind over matter and all those catch phrases about ways to get mentally strong. I remember my coach speaking to the whole team about forgetting the past and learning from mistakes. For me, it all became a reality when I started thinking about my dream car.

It really worked for me to use the rear view mirror and front windshield visualization technique to help put things in perspective. It helped me to gather my thoughts and allow the top half of my brain to reason with all these negative feelings and thoughts that I was experiencing.

The great baseball victory that day and week-long soul searching experience provided a life lesson for me that I could use while going forward. This lesson would help me deal with any situation I may encounter in the future.

As fathers and husbands working full time trying to support families, we all deal with the same pressures in life. We are all trying to juggle so many things like being a good parent, spouse and employee. As a student or a child, you may be trying to deal with pressure from your parents and teachers, but also with peer pressure from your friends.

It does not matter what your age is when it comes to our feelings. We all experience self- doubt and are feeling negative some days. We all make mistakes and sometimes are not happy with the past or the situation that we maybe experiencing presently. We can make a choice on how our attitude will be during these situations. You can chose to look in the rear view mirror and let all the negative thoughts keep you down. If you made a mistake, you can continue to dwell on it or you can look out that front windshield. You can let go of your past and seize the opportunities that may lay in front you.

Life lesson: *When you wake up daily, take a morning walk of gratitude and prayer. It will create a fertile mind ready for success and prepare you for today.*

Stay positive and look out the front windshield all the time. No mater how bad things may seem, remember that you are great and you always have options because when God closes a door he also opens up a window. Learn from the past but try to let it go, become free from your mistakes.

I would like all of you to think about your dream car and imagine yourself driving it. Think of all the happiness these feelings bring to you. Visualization techniques can help get you to a place and can be the first step to becoming mentally stronger. You can now control your emotions and help put things into perspective as you concentrate striving for success. I reflect on that day in the batters box and use that experience to remind myself how I was able to overcome all that stress. It helped shaped my life as an adult preparing me to handle any challenge that I may face.

Life lesson: *If, you feel lost, pray for guidance and God will show you the way*

The next time you step into your own car take a look at that rear view mirror and front windshield. You can decide right then and there how you will chose your attitude that day. You can be positive and look out the front windshield, or remain negative and continue to dwell on the past, hating yourself and your situation by looking through the rear view mirror.

I hope you all find peace and happiness by living your life and fulfilling all your dreams. Stay positive and always look forward. Accept all the challenges that life has in store for you. Find something in your life that you can use as a visualization technique that will help you shed your negative thought patterns. For me, the dream car scenario really worked. It helped keep me cool, calm and collected while under much stress playing in that big baseball game.

Baseball is a team sport, but you are all alone in the batter's box and on the pitcher's mound. It becomes a battle between two athletes who are trying to help their team win. I was fortunate to come out ahead that day and win my battle against that pitcher. The baseball that I hit that day for a triple was fair by about one inch. It could have easily gone the other way and been called foul. I was lucky. Just like in baseball and in life, I believe that we create our own luck and always staying positive is the key to achieving success.

I became so mentally tough that day. I was focused on the task at hand with such positive energy and strong belief in my success that it all came together for our team and me. We won and it felt great. That day we happened to be the better team, a nice drive in my dream car by Len Zen helped to make it all possible.

Life Lesson: *Remember that you may not be driving your dream car but use the one you have for more then just driving. Let it help remind you of all that you can be and achieve. Stay positive and believe in yourself and good things will follow.*

Third Inning

Jacob Becomes Mentally Tough and Learns About The Four C's.

My college baseball career was coming to an end. I enjoyed playing four years and trying to advance my career in the professional ranks. I was not any different from most kids who dream of playing professional baseball.

It was a goal and dream that I set early on in my young life. It appeared that at every level of play, my skills seemed to get better and better with making those adjustments from middle school baseball to high school, and now finishing with a strong career at the college ranks.

The competition became much tougher as I moved up these higher levels of play, but so did my skills. I seemed to grow stronger and get better each year. That is something that you want to see in any athlete as they get older and move up. Is the player showing continued improvement or has the game caught up with them and they begin to lag behind other players?

In college, every year I managed to get better and better each season with hopes of impressing professional scouts and one day signing a contract to play professional baseball. I never did sign that professional baseball contract, so I moved on with my life using my college degree and beginning a career in finance.

Life Lesson: *The lesson I learned from this experience was about adversity. Remember, the best don't just face adversity; they embrace it, knowing it is not a dead end, but a detour to some greater and better things around the corner.*

After working for a few years, I married my wife Susanne, whom I met in college. Within a few months after getting married, we received some exciting news that my wife was pregnant with our first child. On September 29th, our first son was born and we named him Jacob.

It was an exciting time but also a nervous time. My wife and I were going through all these new life experiences in a very short period of time. We just got married, bought our first home and we were now having our first child all within the first year of marriage.

These three life events are considered to be major events and most people spread them out over a period of time.

When you become a parent it seems that everything changes, especially your outlook on life. You want to make sure that you raise your child to be strong and safe. You want to protect the child from harm and provide them with a nice home and community to grow up in.

I began to share with my first son Jacob all the knowledge that I had learned growing up. When he was ready to play sports, I wanted to make sure that he was mentally strong and knew everything about the game, so when it was his time to play he would be ready.

I felt that being mentally strong was just as important as teaching him how to catch, throw, run and hit the baseball. I believe that all athletes at any level need to be mentally strong, because once you allow any doubt and fear to enter your mind it only opens the door for failure. I wanted Jacob to become a complete player with exceptional mental strength. I wanted him to have the ability to block out any pressure situations and clear his mind so that he could focus on the task at hand and succeed for his team and also for himself. Jacob would have to master his thought patterns and find a way to relax so that he could concentrate while performing under a stressful game situation that may arise.

I wanted Jacob to become the smartest kid both on and off the field. I was considered by my college baseball coach to be a highly intelligent baseball player on the field. I would anticipate situations and always knew what to do with the ball before it was hit my way. I always made great decisions on the field and I had what they called a high baseball IQ.

When I played shortstop in college, I was the captain of our infield and would provide signals to the other infield players on options that we would run to defend the other team's offense. The game of baseball is more than just throwing and hitting the ball. It is also like a game of chess where both teams have a strategy and try to outwit each other. You need to be ready to counter every move that they make. People who really understand the game of baseball understand this cat and mouse game that goes on between teams. They can appreciate when a team can make a defensive play to counter the offensive strategy that their opponent had been trying to execute.

The game becomes really exciting when you understand what the other team may be trying to accomplish. The game is also simple in the fact that the team that scores more runs than the other wins. It is the process of getting your players in position to score for your team. If you are mentally strong and understand those situations and don't get nervous when asked to perform in these highly stressful times, some players outperform others. Some defensive players will make mental mistakes when they throw to the wrong base.

Some offensive players strike out when the game is on the line and can't perform in clutch situations. They lack mental toughness and shut down. I had success with a clutch hit with two outs and two strikes in the bottom of the ninth during that big game in college. I believe that my success occurred because I was mentally tough and able to perform in this high-pressure situation. I could have easily let fear enter my mind and shut down, therefore failing in my task by striking out. If I did not block out the pressure of the situation by remaining calm and focused, then we may have lost that big game. This would have cost my team the chance of advancing to the NCAA tournament.

Life Lesson: *When the going gets tough the tough is mentally strong, focused, and in the zone blocking out all distractions from your opponent striving for success.*

We have all heard a coach talk about getting your head in the game. He is referring to exactly what I am saying about being mentally strong. Pressure can affect everyone and the player who can stay calm and focused during those situations is mentally stronger than the others. Mentally strong players thrive in those situations. We have all heard the phrase "*That player choked in that situation.*" Now they are not referring to them as choking on a piece of food, they are really saying that player blew that particular situation for his team. He cracked under the pressure and could not perform.

It could be a professional baseball player in the late innings that only needs one out in order for his team to win the World Series for the first time in decades. A routine ground ball approaches him while playing first base and it goes through his legs, costing his team the series. The player would normally make this simple play 99 out of 100 times but failed that time. It is the pressure of that situation which he was not mentally strong and in that moment lost his focus. He could not clear his mind to focus on the simple task of stopping this routine ground ball. In return, he got embarrassed and cost his team the World Series.

It could happen to any of us. These are the types of situations that I wanted to share with my son Jacob and help prepare him to handle the pressure, so that he could make the play and help his team win. I was also trying to prevent him from making a mistake and having him avoid the embarrassment, if he ever was in that situation. As a parent, we all try to help prepare our kids for life and everything that it throws at them. I was being a little over the top when educating Jacob about sports and life, but felt the more knowledge I could share with him the better prepared he would be. The rest would be up to him to make the right decisions and come out on top for himself and his team.

Life Lesson: *When you are in a high-pressure situation and the game is on the line and everyone is watching you, remember to smile, have fun, and enjoy it. Life is short; you only live once. You have nothing to lose. Seize the moment and you will treasure the memory.*

Being mentally tough can help you to succeed in the classroom, athletic fields, workplace and in life. Once Jacob started to walk and still in diapers, I began teaching him how to play sports, I still remember buying him his first baseball glove and basketball. While Jacob was sitting down on the floor one morning, we noticed that he would naturally pick up blocks and toys with his left hand. This was the first time that I knew he would throw left-handed. While I was out shopping for his new baseball glove, I made sure to pick up the proper glove to fit him and help get him ready as a left handed baseball player.

Jacob enjoyed baseball and we would play catch every day. He liked swinging the baseball bat, so I would throw pitches to him so he could hit. I would teach Jacob so he would be able to hit from both sides of the plate, both left and right handed. Jacob was only two years old when we started playing catch every day. I would use a tennis ball so that it would not hurt him if he missed the ball and it hit his face. This is also a great ball to use when teaching a child how to catch fly balls. If he missed one and it plunked him on the head it would not hurt.

Life Lesson: *Use a wiffle or tennis ball while teaching a young child to learn how to play catch for baseball and softball so they won't get hurt if they miss the ball and it hits them.*

Jacob was now getting older and beginning to play organized baseball and basketball in our local town leagues. He began playing baseball at the age of five. Jacob and his cousin Sean had a great time playing together on the same team. I recommend that all of you invest in a camcorder and begin filming your child when they start playing sports at this age. The footage is priceless as you get to watch your child as they learn and grow while playing the game. This is also a time that they understand the importance of playing together as a team. Along with making new friends, it is a wonderful time being out there on the baseball field.

For me, it felt like my life had come full circle. I was out on that same little league field that I grew up playing baseball on, and I was now coaching my son Jacob. I had a blast teaching him the greatest game on earth, our national pastime, **BASEBALL**. Over the years, I would take the time to teach Jacob all about the game of baseball and the different situations that go on in the game. As a left-handed player, the number of positions for him to play was limited. This was fine, and I would spend most of my time teaching him all about those positions that he would eventually grow into.

Life Lesson: *Enjoy the time you take teaching your child to play sports and have patience.*

You never have a left-handed baseball or softball player at third base, shortstop, second base or catcher. These types of players are limited to playing the outfield, first base or pitching. I would get Jacob excited about playing the outfield and have fun teaching him how to catch fly balls properly. I wanted Jacob to be prepared to be able to play any of these positions. I knew very well from my own experiences playing baseball, as Jacob got older and better at playing more positions, the better chance he would have at making the high school team. Even though Jacob was only five years old at the time, I was already preparing him for high school. I always look ten years out and plan ahead so why not get Jacob thinking the same way.

From the ages of five through twelve, I would begin to help Jacob become mentally stronger as well as physically better at the game of baseball. I would spend time with him explaining all the game situations that he could possibly face and the strategies teams will try to use during the game. I taught him how to catch fly balls, knowing one day he may end up only being able to play in the outfield. Every child needs to work on this. Being able to catch fly balls and line drives is most important at every position. It is also the best way to keep your child safe while playing baseball.

Kids today are hitting the baseball and softball harder and faster, especially with the advanced technology of the bats they are being supplied with. Every parent needs to understand that kids need to be really good at catching the ball and getting the glove in position to stop the ball from hitting them in the face and head. The child needs to always pay attention while on the field because the balls move very quickly towards them.

I started off slowly using a tennis ball to help Jacob learn how to catch fly balls and line drives right at his face. He needed to know how to turn his glove properly to catch the line drive while it is coming at his face so he would not get hurt. Safety was the first and most important feature while educating Jacob about the game of baseball. I knew that I could not always be out there for him and he would have to do it alone. I figured that it was best to prepare him to defend himself and protect himself while playing baseball. While in the batter's box, it is important for the player to turn his body away from a pitch if it approaches his or her body especially there face. They want to make sure that they turn there head away from the pitch and if they get hit it will be in a safer location on the body.

Jacob did not like to get hit in the face with the tennis ball but he soon realized that it was a lot easier and less painful than a baseball. Jacob quickly learned how to protect his face by turning his glove the proper way when a ball was coming right towards his face. He would also learn the best way to turn his body in the batter's box to protect his face and chest.

Life Lesson: *Safety is first. Make sure your child has the proper equipment and skill set.*

Jacob enjoyed learning how to catch and play the outfield. I explained to him that being left-handed limited him on being able to play certain positions. He really had no choice and the odds were that he could end up playing in the outfield. I don't know why kids today do not like to play the outfield .It is where most of the action is. The majority of professional baseball players in the Hall of Fame played in the outfield. I recommend that all kids learn how to catch line drives and fly balls and play all three positions in the outfield first, prior to moving them into the infield.

I would not even let my child play in the infield until he was good at catching the ball. The simple fact is that while playing in the infield you are closer to the batter and the ball will travel faster to you than if you are in the outfield. Your teammates are also closer and when they throw the ball to you it is important that you can catch it.

I still remember a mom complaining that her child could never play first base on Jacob's team when they were younger. The mom did not understand that we were looking out for her child's safety because he could not catch. At every practice, we were trying to teach him how to catch. We were hoping that eventually he could play in the position that he loved, which was first base, but it took time. She would complain that he was always in the outfield and I would explain to her our concerns for his safety. I also asked if she, his father, or another sibling would work with him everyday at home practicing catching the ball. We only had the child for an hour for practice twice a week. He needed to practice on his own at home, just like when you have to do homework after school.

She said that they did not have any time to practice with the child at home and why couldn't we just put the child at first base because they paid for him to play just like everyone else. The mom was making a big scene yelling that only the coach's kid gets to play the good positions and her kid is always stuck in the outfield.

We agreed to put the child out there at first base the next inning. Now understand that at first base you have the ball thrown at you from every other position in the infield. The ball comes at you from all different angles and it is not the easiest position to play.

You need to be able to catch the ball well and get your feet aligned around the first base bag and with the runner coming down the base path right towards you, it can be distracting. The first ball thrown to him came from our third basemen and he could throw the ball very hard. It went right to the boy standing on first base. The boy did not turn his glove correctly and caught the ball with his face. It hit him straight in the mouth, knocking out all his front teeth and breaking his nose.

Life Lesson: *Be realistic with your child while encouraging them to play sports. Listen to the coach, especially when safety is a concern.*

The poor boy was screaming and there was blood everywhere. We called for the ambulance and the frantic mom came running. The mom looked at me, not taking any blame for demanding that we put him out there. My worst fear was realized and of course the mom blamed me for the accident. That boy never played baseball again and his career was over at the age of seven. I felt terrible about the child getting hurt but the good news was he fully recovered and joined the school band. He was a great kid and nice to have around. If his parents could have been a little more patient as we worked with the child, he probably would have been ready to play the position of his choice later that year. That poor child and his parents had to learn a tough life lesson the hard way. These are the same type of parents who always complain and are negative all the time to the coaching staff. They somehow feel that their child is intentionally being left out, especially when selecting the all-star teams. These negative parents will always say that the coach's kid made the all-star team but why not their child? They think it is politics, but in the end it is having the best-prepared kids who can represent the town who make the all-star team.

Do these negative people ever stop and think that maybe the reason why the coach's kid does make the all-star team is because the coach has that child outside seven days week practicing for hours on all facets of the game?

Life lesson: *When you face negative people, know that the key to life is to stay positive in the face of negativity, not in the absence of it. After all, everyone will have to overcome negativity to define him or her and create his or her own success.*

I spent so much time with Jacob preparing him to avoid this type of baseball accident. We would be outside in the cold because we live in the northeast and as much as he hated those cold days, Jacob knew in the end it was helping him. I was always honest with Jacob about his skills. I set realistic expectations about sports and his abilities to perform in certain positions on the field. Teach your child to appreciate and love the game and enjoy the time they spend with their friends. The odds are not in their favor that they will go any further than making the high school team and if they do, it is a great accomplishment. There is so much talent out there so try and keep expectations realistic and support your child's efforts. Support them when they succeed but also if they fail. Keep their spirits up and always offer positive words of encouragement.

Life Lesson: *Any bad day you have, I recommend you stop and get an ice cream cone. Take your child and it could be the greatest life lesson of all no words needed.*

Jacob would become very knowledgeable about baseball and had a good understanding on what to do with the baseball prior to it being hit his way. He became a very good outfielder, first baseman, and pitcher. He understood all the game situations and how to make the right decision with the play. I felt comfortable with Jacob catching the ball and began to work with him more as a pitcher. I explained to him all about this position and the importance of moving the ball to certain locations on the plate. Pitching is not just about rearing back and trying to throw fastballs by the batter.

Having a great fastball is important, but if that is your only pitch then the batter will make adjustments. He will begin to have success against you and start hitting the ball out of the park. The pitcher needs to have the ability to change the speed of the ball and move it to different locations on the plate. As a pitcher, the main goal is to keep the batter off balance and keep the batter guessing on your next pitch. When the pitcher is effective by changing speeds and locations of the ball, it makes the batter uncomfortable and gets them to make outs. There is a difference between a thrower and a pitcher. A thrower just rear backs and throws as hard as they can, trying to blow the ball by the batter. The pitcher is smart and will use all his different types of pitches such as a fastball, changeup, curve ball, slider, knuckleball, and spot the ball on different locations of the plate to be successful.

Jacob had a good understanding about the game and all the different situations that may occur on the baseball field. I felt good about his progress and every year he got taller and stronger. Now I started to begin training Jacob all about being mentally tough.

In every sport, the physical skills of an athlete are important. The next phase of training for Jacob was the mental toughness that he needed to learn about so that he would be prepared to handle any pressure situation. The next set of skills that I began to teach Jacob about becoming mentally tough were skills that I felt that would help him not only on the baseball fields, but also in the classroom and later on in life when he entered the work force.

I called these the **Four C's** of becoming mentally tough. They are **C**onfidence, **C**ourage, **C**ompetitiveness and **C**ontinued Improvement.

Confidence is all about you believing in yourself, your skills and your abilities. When you step on the baseball field, basketball court, or any sport venue you love, remind yourself that you are the best. There is nobody better than you. You need to block out the opponent and the crowd who may support your opponent by booing you.

You need to take your mind to a place where you feel strong and do not listen to any negative words, as it is a trick to make you feel weak. This could allow your mind to start doubting your skills and abilities.

The reason why sports teams love playing at home is they yearn for the extra support they get from the home crowd cheering them on.

The home crowd provides support and will help to boost the confidence in the athlete. This support and confidence from the home crowd will make the athlete feel stronger and help them to believe that they can accomplish anything. You need to understand that having **confidence in yourself** is all that you need to be a successful athlete, student, and employee.

The other team has to deal with a thousand people who may be booing them and it is quite intimidating. The mentally tough person will block it all out and focus on himself by constantly reminding himself that he is the best. If you are a member of a team, focus on doing your job. If everyone does just that, then together you will find success.

As a team member, you cannot think about doing it all by yourself. That becomes an unrealistic expectation and now you are putting too much pressure on yourself. This, along with the hostile crowd, will allow your mind to begin to cave in and negative thoughts will distract you. This can ultimately lead you to make mistakes and failing in your job duties as the team member.

We all hear the phrase that "He is in the zone." **The zone** is a place in your mind where you are constantly reminding yourself that you are the best and you have all the confidence you need. If you make a mistake, you need to forget it immediately because you cannot change the outcome. It is over with and it is important to begin building your confidence again by saying you are the best, staying positive and moving forward with your task at hand.

We would all love to have that big crowd cheering us on and providing that extra support, but that is unrealistic. In the end, the mentally tough person does not need the cheering crowd to be successful. He or she has conditioned himself or herself to becoming self-confident. He or she relies on himself or she to keep their mind focused, and with the support of their coach, boss, teammates, or work colleagues, they can win in any situation.

Confidence is also important for having success in the classroom or at work when you are done playing sports and trying to support your family. The same rules apply. Remind yourself that you are the best student or employee. **You must believe in order to achieve.** If you don't believe in yourself then is it not realistic for someone else to believe in you.

Life Lesson: *Play with no fear and always remain confident in every situation*

Courage is having the heart of a champion and **playing without fear or doubt.** You are not afraid of the opponent or the hostile crowd that maybe cheering them on and booing you every time you step on the field. **Courage** is all about showing up and doing your best to help your team succeed. A person in the boxing ring who keeps getting knocked down but still keeps getting up has courage. He or she never quits. No matter how bad the situation seems and with all the odds stacked up against you, **never quit**. Have the courage to always keep working hard and fighting back to help reach your goal and win.

I have come across too many kids today who quit when things don't seem to go their way. They make all kinds of excuses and want to blame everyone else for their shortcomings. You may never like every situation while playing a sport. If you worked hard and made the team, then it is important to continue to show up and stick with that commitment until the end. When you enter the workplace, I guarantee you that you will not like something. It could be your boss or another co-worker, so what are you going to then, just quit? That can be difficult, especially if you need the money to support your family. You need to have the courage to keep showing up and performing your duties. Find peace by staying positive everyday.

I taught Jacob that if you begin to quit one thing, then as you get older in life it becomes too easy to start quitting everything when things don't seem to go your way. It is not a good way to live and you never want to be considered as a quitter. You need to have the courage to work through the tough situations. Compromise and sacrifice for the betterment of the team.

Life Lesson: *Quitting at a young age turns into a bad habit. You begin to quit as an adult when things get tough at work. Avoid forming bad habits.*

Courage is what people have who do not allow anyone or anything negative to enter their mind. They know that once it does, they are only giving in and are on the path of self-destruction. Once you allow any negative thoughts or self-doubt to enter your mind, then you will fail. You cannot allow anyone to intimidate you because it will lead to failure. Negative thoughts lead to Fear and self-doubt and eventually failure of the task.

If you think that you are going to fail, then you probably will. It is important for you to continue to believe in yourself and as the going gets tough the tough get going. We all have heard that many times but it is true. It is up to you to dig deep and keep working towards your goal. Fear is the number one feeling that can cripple an athlete or anyone trying to accomplish anything while playing sports, doing schoolwork or in the workplace. The fear of losing, failure, looking foolish, and rejection are all negative feelings and lead to losing. Fear can consume you and the best athlete can look like a below average player because he has allowed fear to enter into his mind.

The person who has courage will not allow his mind to even go there and never think about these negative thoughts. If they do set in, then only you can find the courage to fight back and remind yourself that win or lose, you will always do your best. We all have the courage to be successful in sports, school and the work place, so just go for it.

Life Lesson: *Courage means that you will show up and try your best. Win or lose understand that you have taken a big step by coming forward and find gratification in all that you attempt. In the movie the "Wizard Of OZ" the lion found the courage to show up and ask for a heart. In the end he came to realize he had one all along but he only needed to believe in himself.*

Competitiveness is having a strong desire to win in sports, the classroom and in life. Once you have the confidence and courage to show up, then take it one step further and work hard to win. As an athlete, student and employee you have invested your time and energy working hard towards a goal. What is the point of writing down your goals and then working hard everyday towards them and not wanting to win? I have met so many people who really don't care about winning. Winning is about finishing something that you started and finding success from that accomplishment. It is all about putting your best foot forward and trying to win.

If you are a student in class working hard, taking notes from your teacher and studying for a test, then **win** the best grade you can get. You have done all the work. Relax, during the test have the confidence and courage to show up and win. You are going to appreciate yourself and those efforts will be rewarded.

As the president of our local baseball little league, we are teaching the children about the importance of playing fair, working together, and winning. We are trying to prepare these youngsters not only for the game, but also for life. The same values that they learn on the ball field, working together for a common goal, can be found in every corporation in America. We are not teaching the children about winning at all costs which could entail berating and booing the other team, disrespecting the game, and being a poor sport. We want them to play hard and strive to win but win or lose, appreciate your accomplishment.

Parents always say to me while I was the president, "Why can't it just be all about having fun and no winning?" I never met a child who was just having fun by losing everyday. It is all about having a balance and a strong desire to win by giving the child the tools necessary to prepare them to win, and then sending them out there with the team as they try to accomplish just that together as a group.

Do we really want to prepare our children by teaching them about the importance of working hard together as a team towards one goal and then say it is okay if you don't win? They will then think it is okay not to win in the game of life. They will grow up thinking that they don't deserve to win and will never have that desire to be competitive.

I have a friend who ran a twenty-six mile marathon and did not come in first place. In his mind he won because he was able to run for twenty-six miles without stopping. That is a great accomplishment and I believe he is a winner. He had the confidence and courage to show up and was competitive by accomplishing a monumental goal.

You should be competitive in everything that you set out to do in school, work, and athletics. Stay positive, have confidence and courage in yourself, and strive towards being competitive as you win in the game of life.

Life Lesson: *Play to win and remember that you're only as good as your last performance. Learn from it and make adjustments while you improve next time.*

Continued Improvement is having the ability to understand that no matter how good you think you are, there is always room for improvement. The very best athletes in the world are never satisfied and are always working harder to improve their craft. They know that somebody is always working harder to take their spot.

I teach my boys that when you tryout for a sport, everyone works hard during that process to make the team. Once you make the team, then every practice and every game must be played with the same intensity you put forth in the tryout. You cannot rest and celebrate just because you made the team. You will now need to work harder then you did during the tryout so you can become a starter and play in the game. If you become a starter on the team then you need to step it up another notch and keep working hard because great athletes never give up. Somebody who is mentally stronger will keep working, trying to take your spot. That is competition and you must continue to improve and work harder then everyone else around you to keep what you have earned.

A coach will always watch how the athlete performs in practice and that helps them decide on who will start and play in the games. They use the practice as a testing area so it is important for you to always practice hard. If you work as hard at every practice the same way that you did that day in the tryout, you will have success and play for that team in the games. I have seen too many young athletes work hard during the tryout, make the team, and then they goof around at every practice. They wonder why the coach will not play them in the game. The parents will then complain to the coach that their kid never plays. I bet that coach wished he had a videotape to show what that player did every practice.

Life Lesson: *Practice what you preach, never stop working to perfect your craft?*

The elite athlete knows that he or she can always improve and is willing to listen to a coach or parent who may have noticed a flaw in their game. Working on this flaw will help the athlete become even better. Some athletes cannot accept criticism and demonstrate a poor attitude when approached with any suggestions for improvement. This can be detrimental to the athlete in the long run because other players who are willing to accept the idea of *continued improvement* will catch up to you and eventually surpass your skills and take your job. We all should embrace the concept of **continued improvement** in our lives by always striving to perform better.

As an employee, I am always looking for ways to improve my craft as a salesperson. I keep an open mind when our corporation makes changes. They are trying to help us all improve and have success when helping our customers. I know that by learning new ideas and techniques they are only helping me to grow as a person and becoming a better employee.

Life Lesson: *open your mind to change and accept positive critics, as it will help you improve your skill set and springs you towards success.*

Teachers in school are working hard daily trying to reach all the students in class by educating them on a certain subject. As a student, you should embrace this and understand that continued improvement is happening every day for you in all your classes. Your knowledge in any particular subject is much better at the end of the school year than it was on the first day.

I spent a lot of time working with my son Jacob helping him to become mentally stronger by understanding each and every one of the **four C's**. *Continued improvement* is something that Jacob embraced and over time his skills and abilities in sports improved. His confidence, courage and competitive spirit in the classroom would propel him to the number one ranked student in his class. He applied the **four C's** both in the classroom and on the athletic fields and found success.

Life Lesson: *Be a good sport; stay competitive and always strive to win in all that you do.*

Jacob was now eight years old and playing for a championship in our local Little League program. Jacob was a left-handed pitcher and first basemen. He had become a good student of the game, achieving a high baseball IQ. He would have to use each and every one of these **four C's** that I had been teaching him his whole life as the championship game began. It was the last Little League baseball game of the season and happened to be the championship game. During the first few years of Jacob's young baseball career, he was considered to be a below average pitcher. He did not have the strongest pitching arm in the league but he had great control and understood how to pitch.

Jacob was asked to come into the championship game and **pitch** with the **bases loaded** and nobody out in the bottom of the last inning. At the time, Jacob and his team were winning by one run and this was the other teams last chance at bat. They had their rally caps on and their fans were cheering for their team, hoping to come back and win the championship.

Jacob took the mound and with all the parents watching and all this pressure on him, he tried to shut the other team down. He began to throw his warm-up pitches to home plate. The crowd was large and all the parents started getting into the game by cheering for their respective team. The other team was laughing at Jacob while he was warming up. The reason why they were laughing was Jacob did not throw the baseball very fast from the pitcher's mound to home plate. Jacob knew it but he never let that bother him while he prepared himself to battle the other team's top hitters.

The other team did not demonstrate good sportsmanship by laughing at another team's player, and they were reminded to keep it cool by cheering on their own player. They were trying to intimidate Jacob and make him feel weak, so they would have a better chance of succeeding and winning the game. They were trying to intimidate and instill fear into Jacob.

Life Lesson: *Whenever you fear, trust. Let your faith be greater than your doubt, believe in yourself and always have confidence in all that you attempt to accomplish.*

Jacob would have to dig deep and call upon all the confidence, courage, and competitive spirit he could muster. He needed to keep his head in the game, staying mentally strong and performing to best of his abilities in this high-pressure game situation.

I watched Jacob very closely from the sidelines and could tell that he was entering into the ***zone*** as he went about his business warming up. At the time, he would be facing the best hitters in the league.

In that situation Jacob had the perfect mindset and skills to deliver strikes, giving our team the best chance to make a play in the field and hopefully win the game. If he walked a batter he would give up the game tying run and he had to avoid doing just that.

Life lesson: *If, you feel distracted, focus on your breathing, observe your surroundings, clear your mind and get into the zone. The zone is not a random event. It can be created with confidence, courage and a strong desire to win.*

I gave Jacob a lot of credit for coming into the game during that situation and he had a lot of courage after he had to listen to the other team laughing as he warmed up. It takes a lot of guts for an eight-year old to take the mound with all that pressure riding on him in the bottom of the inning, playing for a championship game.

The umpire called for the next hitter to get into the batter's box and yelled out " *Play ball.*" This was it and Jacob reared back, threw the first pitch with no swing from the batter and the umpired yelled out "Strike one."

Our team went crazy and everyone seemed to get a boost of confidence after Jacob delivered that first pitch for a strike. The next pitch came and the batter took a mighty swing and missed the ball completely for strike two. Jacob was feeling more and more confident with each pitch. Jacob got the ball and then threw the next pitch and the batter took another mighty swing unsuccessfully for **strike three."** Batters out" yelled the umpire. Jacob had just successfully thrown three pitches past one of the best hitters in the league. The other team was now beginning to quiet down as our team was roaring with applause.

The umpire called for the next hitter to enter the batter's box and Jacob was beaming with confidence after he struck out the first hitter and getting one out. Jacob knew he could not celebrate because they still needed two more outs and he had much work to do. Jacob went into his wind up and delivered the pitch while the batter swung and missed the ball for **strike one**. The crowd was going crazy as Jacob took the ball and began to deliver the second pitch. The hitter did not swing and it was on the outside corner and the umpire yelled, "**Strike two**."

Life Lesson: *while playing sports keep your cool and head in the game until the final out and victory is at hand don't celebrate to early.*

Nine Innings

The batter was very upset. He stepped out of the batter's box and could feel the pressure mounting on him as he now had two strikes. The batter took a couple practice swings, looked down at his coach for a boost of confidence, and then got back in there to face the pitcher.

Jacob, knowing that he had the advantage with two strikes and no balls on the batter, decided to throw a waste pitch. This is a pitch that is low and away from the hitter and you hope they will take the bait and swing at a bad pitch. It worked out perfectly because the hitter swung at a low pitch in the dirt, **striking out,** making the second out of the game.

Jacob had just successfully struck out the first two batters and now they were only one out away from winning the Little League championship game. The crowd was going crazy and all the momentum and confidence seemed to shift from the other team to ours. Jacob just struck out two of the best hitters in the league and they were one out away from winning the little league championship.

The next hitter approached the batter's box. The hitter took his practice swings. He was the best hitter on their team. He took his time and then looked down to his coach standing near third base, looking for the signals. The coach told him to swing away and offered some words of encouragement. Jacob was very close to helping his team win the championship game. He had just struck out the first two batters he faced and now was facing the best hitter not only on the other team, but also in the whole league. This hitter had more home runs then anyone in the league and had three hits already for this game. Jacob delivered the first pitch and the batter swung as hard as he could. He completely missed the ball for **strike one**. The hitter, getting frustrated, slammed his bat and banged it on the plate and stepped out of the batter's box.

The hitter looked down to the coach and was reminded to keep his head and stay cool. He had two more chances with only one strike on him. The hitter got back into the batter's box and Jacob delivered the next pitch low and away with another unsuccessful swing, "**Strike two**," yelled the umpire.

The crowd was going crazy while everyone cheered and jumped up and down. Jacob and his team were all feeling great. They only need one more strike to upset this team and win the championship. It was not that long ago when the other team was laughing at Jacob as he warmed up. The other team was silent and they all seemed to lose hope even though the game was still not over. Jacob had used his mental toughness blocked out the other team booing and focused. Jacob could not throw the ball fast but used his skills pitching intelligently and moving the ball around the strike zone keeping these hitters off balance and confused.

The hitter was very upset and nervous as he looked down to his coach for support and a boost of confidence. The coach tried to encourage him but I could see the fear in the batters eyes. His body language demonstrated the fear as he had his head down and shoulders were slumped over a clear signal of somebody not feeling very confident.

The umpire yelled, "Play ball!" and instructed the hitter to get back in the batter's box. Jacob took the baseball, went into his wind up and delivered the next pitch. Jacob would muster all his strength, rear back and throw a fastball right past the batter for **strike three**. The batter was puzzled as he was looking for a waste pitch considering that there were two strikes on him and that is what Jacob did to the last batter by throwing the ball low and away in the dirt when he had two strikes on the other batter. Jacob changed tactics and decided to throw this next and final pitch right down the middle and out smarted the batter. The gamble for Jacob worked and he struck this batter out.

Life Lesson: *Believe and trust your skills using your intelligence to help win.*

The game was over and Jacob and his team successfully won the Little League championship game. Against all odds, they upset the best team in the league that year. Jacob, who was laughed at, and was not the hardest throwing pitcher managed to pitch his team to victory.

Jacob applied the mind over matter principle. It was at that moment in time that I realized Jacob applied the **Four C's** that I had been drilling into his head over the first seven years of his life. He was mentally stronger than everyone else at the field that day, including all the spectators. He was able to block out all the laughter the other team had applied trying to discourage and make Jacob feel weak while he was warming up but that tactic did not work.

Life Lesson: *Use the **four C's** and you will find success in school, sports, work, and life.*

Jacob had the **c**onfidence to believe in himself and his own skills. He had the **c**ourage to step on the pitcher's mound all by himself in a high-pressure situation and face the best hitters in the league. He had the **c**ompetitive spirit and desire to play and **win** the championship game and worked so hard over those previous seven years, accepting the notion of **c**ontinued improvement and never gave up.

It was a perfect example of how anyone can achieve success in sports and in life. I want all of you to think about the **four C's** and use them in your life and remember that you must believe in order to achieve. If an eight year old could overcome all those odds, then I believe that you can too.

My wife Susanne and I were blessed with a second child. A second son was born on June 15 and we named him Joshua. I would then begin my journey of teaching these same lessons all over again to help prepare Joshua.

Life Lesson: *Share your knowledge with family and friends, become a mentor.*

Josh, who is four years younger then Jake, would learn much more quickly because he wanted to keep up with his big older brother. Josh was so much more advanced in athletics at an earlier age than Jacob ever was.

At the age of eight, Joshua was good enough to make and play little league. This is rare because the youngest player I had ever seen try out and make this league was nine years old. Josh would outdo his big brother in little league, helping his team to win three little league championships in four years. Josh would also become mentally strong and have a high baseball IQ.

We are proud of them and are looking forward to watching them both play for the high school team. I hope you all try to use the **four C's** in your life and find success. We all need to have confidence and courage, striving to be competitive and winning in the game of life.

We can embrace continued improvement by reading books on a regular basis and studying harder, getting more proficient in our jobs. There are many people who are willing to learn more and work harder to keep up with us.

We live in the greatest country in the world, the land of opportunity. This is a place where we encourage people to be creative and use the skills and abilities that God gave us to make a better life for our families and ourselves. Seize this opportunity to shine and embrace greatness. I believe in all of you and ask that you help yourself by always taking on every challenge with **Confidence**, **Courage**, and a **Competitive** spirit to win. You will have success and understand that a stumble or failure is no excuse to quit.

It is at those darkest moments in your life when you must dig deep and find the strength to **continue to improve** yourself and the lives of others around you. You are an inspiration and a winner. Life is never easy and sometimes doing things the hard way offers the greatest life lesson of all. It teaches us to appreciate hard work and the satisfaction you receive for doing a good job and accomplishing something that maybe you never thought you had the courage to complete.

You can master your thoughts and when you're feeling negative and against all odds, use the inner strength to fight through. Always stay positive and work toward the goals that you set. You all have the ability to become mentally stronger and independent. The **four C's** are here as a guide helping you to achieve success today and tomorrow. Be brave and embrace change and try to get out of your comfort zone.

If you continue to make the same mistakes and are not willing to try something different to change your situation then you will only continue to fail. You have absolutely nothing to lose to try and make a change for the better. If you apply the **four C's** then your attitude will improve and your behaviors will change and you may just find the spark that you were looking for leading to a more positive outcome for you.

Life Lesson: *Nothing ventured then nothing gained.*

Fourth Inning

Joshua Stops Procrastinating

It is my belief that everyone at one time or another hits that snooze button when the alarm goes off at five a.m., waking you up to get ready for work or school. Some people may have hit that snooze button two and three times. It is only natural for all of us to want to roll over in bed and catch up with more sleep.

Procrastination is that snooze alarm and that is how most of us begin our day. I think we should change the name from snooze alarm to the *procrastination* button. In reality, it is exactly what we are all doing so why not call it what it really is. We all begin our day with a negative thought when we hit that button.

We are telling ourselves that we don't want to get up and tackle the business of today. We begin this thought process in our mind that I believe to be a negative start to our day and it can carry on and affect our attitude. I know that it may sound silly and we are only delaying the start of our day by hitting the procrastination button for two minutes.

That two-minute delay is the first test of the day and the first thought. We usually follow it with a negative comment. We might say " I don't want to go to school today" or "I don't want to go to work today." Has anyone out there ever said those words? I would guess that we probably all did at one time or another in our life.

We are starting the day with hesitation and negative comments and then our wonderful brain begins to act. We have just shaped our whole outlook for that day with a negative thought, and not a positive one around it. Our attitude towards today is certainly not a positive one. When you say that you don't want to do something but you have no choice and actually have to do it, like go to work or school, then you are going to act miserable when performing that task.

It is only natural for all of us to feel negative when we say that we don't want to do something. The mind is only processing how we feel, and those commands lead to our body language, which is directly affected by those commands.

My younger son Joshua is like any other normal twelve-year old boy who does not want to do a lot of things. Josh will start every day with hitting the *procrastination* button several times. He complains that he does not want to go to school today and every day when he wakes up.

Life lesson: *We can choose our attitude and if so then let's make it be a positive one.*

My wife begins her day arguing with Josh as she tries to get him out of bed. After further thought, we think that Josh skipped right past hitting that procrastination button several times and went right for hitting the **off** button. Josh made up his mind that he was not getting up and that was it.

Josh likes to test those boundaries with his mom and dad. We all know who wins in the end and it is mom. Josh has no choice because he is getting up. Whether he likes it or not, his mom said he has to go to school. When I was growing up, I heard my mom say that exact same phrase every day just like my wife says to Josh.

I take all the blame because our kids do inherit certain traits from their parents and I was a lot like Josh growing up. I did not enjoy going to school and doing a lot of those things all of us kids have to do while growing up. I would also complain about everything, and at the time had no idea how it would affect my attitude for that day.

One day I noticed that Josh was a lot like me and complained about everything that my wife and I would ask him to do every day. As parents, we all teach our kids about the basic necessities in life. We all agree that it is important to eat three meals a day, brush your teeth at least twice a day, go to school and shower daily.

We love our kids and felt that these were the basic necessities and non-negotiable tasks that both our kids would embrace and do without an argument. Josh looked at it completely differently. He agreed they were important and he would do them every day but only on his terms. Josh wanted to do them when he was ready.

Josh, like most kids, loves to play video games, baseball and basketball. He only wanted to do the fun stuff every day and we provided him with plenty of time to do just that. Josh would never argue when we would let him do all the fun stuff. All those arguments would come later when it was time for fun to end and take care of business.

Josh could not find the time with his busy fun schedule to work in all the other basic necessities such as eating, brushing his teeth, going to school or taking a shower. We were intruding on all the fun time that Josh had already conditioned his mind to accept and that was it.

Josh is a lot like me while I was growing up. You may probably have a Josh in your household or know one just like him. I want everyone to know that Josh is a very nice kindhearted kid and loves people. He treats everyone with respect. He has a brilliant mind and I believe that he could be a straight A student if he only applied himself.

I love Joshua with all my heart. The fatherly wisdom and guidance that I shared with Jacob is the same advice that I shared with his younger brother Josh. I realized that they both were different in how they would listen and accept the teachings from both his mom and me.

Life Lesson: *Everyone can improve on our listening skills. Try and become a more active listener and it may help you perform better in school, sports, work and life.*

I needed to find a way to help Joshua understand that his negative thoughts were shaping his day. Josh would need to change his mindset and thought processes, so that he would be the one making those choices of completing the basic necessities in life, and not his mom or dad telling him that he had to do it.

Our oldest son Jacob was much easier because he would always listen and follow his parents' commands without a fuss. Jacob was much quieter and did less talking. He was like a sponge absorbing all the fatherly advice. Jacob knew that this knowledge, if applied, would help him become successful in school and in life.

Jacob found success early in life as a straight A student and as a child who never got into any trouble at school or at home. My wife and I can't remember the last time that we had to yell at Jacob to do anything. We would ask once and he would not hesitate or complain and get up and get it done. His teachers would praise the same behavior when we visited with them at the parent teacher conferences.

Jacob is a perfectionist who is competitive both on the athletic fields and in the classroom. Jacob had earned a reputation in town as a highly intelligent child, well mannered, courteous and a conscientious person. His teachers all adored him and considered him a poster child for being the best student athlete.

Joshua would have a tough road ahead following in the footsteps of his older brother. All that Jacob was able to achieve in school and on the athletic fields set the bar very high. My wife and I wanted our children to simply do their best and we would support each of them no matter what grade they received.

I was never the best student and I never took my schoolwork that seriously. As I look back it probably is one of the only things that I do regret in my life. I should have been a better student and studied more and got good grades while attending high school.

Joshua would follow in my footsteps and begin to get in trouble frequently at school and developed a reputation as a class clown. Joshua would talk out in class. This would result in him get warnings from the teacher, which led to detentions. Usually after the third week of school each year, my wife and I would visit all the teachers.

We would all meet to discuss Joshua as the teachers could detect early on that he was fooling around too much, not listening and disrupting the class. Over a five-year period Joshua would begin to earn a reputation as a student who was falling behind and was being mischievous. We met the school guidance counselor and all the teachers.

Life lesson: *God gave you two ears and one mouth for a reason. You learn more by listening than talking.*

As parents, we were concerned and ready to support Joshua and help him in anyway possible so that he could improve in school and refrain from acting like a class clown.

The school would begin the process of evaluating Joshua for Attention Deficit Hyperactivity Disorder otherwise known as ADHD.

ADHD is a scary phrase. After hearing about it for the first time, I remember my wife and me being a little nervous that Joshua had some fatal disease. It is not, and apparently millions of children and adults suffer from it. I am not an expert on this topic and I am only sharing this story with all of you as an attempt to help Joshua and all the wonderful people just like him.

The test came back and my wife and I were back at the school for yet another meeting with all the teachers, guidance counselor and school psychologist. I want to say that Joshua is very fortunate to grow up in a community and school system that does care and recognize children with possible learning disabilities.

My wife and I support the teachers and the school, appreciating all the time and effort they put into taking this test with Joshua. They were trying to determine if he did have ADHD. The results revealed that Joshua is considered extremely highly intelligent. His answers were off the grid on some questions that were asked of him, and then below average on some of the others.

The school psychologist mentioned that she had never seen scores so high on some of those questions that were asked during the testing process, but was concerned that he was below average on others. The school determined that Joshua had characteristics of ADHD and felt best if we would agree to put him on an IEP.

The Individualized Education Program is a customized learning program designed to get a student extra help during the day. The student could be placed in a classroom where they had two teachers. Joshua could get some one-on-one teaching which would help to keep him organized and on task.

My wife and I were in complete agreement and excited about the school wanting to offer extra help because Joshua was falling behind with his schoolwork. My wife would spend every day after school with Joshua going over his homework and helping him study until ten p.m., and it was exhausting for both of them. We felt Joshua could use the extra help at school.

The other recommendation for students who may suffer from ADHD is to put them on medication. This was the time when my wife and I looked at each other and said "Hold on here, we are not comfortable doing that." My wife and I both agreed that we needed to meet Joshua's primary care pediatrician for his guidance and his medical opinion.

Joshua had the best medical care and we valued the opinions of his doctor. His pediatrician decided that it was best for us to meet with a psychiatrist who specialized in this area. This would help us gain a better understanding of the school's test results. The school has a psychologist but that is different from a psychiatrist.

Our heads were spinning as my wife and I tried to understand the difference between a psychologist and a psychiatrist. A psychiatrist is a doctor who can prescribe medicine and is a specialist in dealing with the mind. We found one who has worked with children for the past thirty years.

Joshua, Susanne and I would meet with this doctor for a two-hour session. The good doctor would spend the time explaining to Joshua and us all about his experience and how he is here to help children who may suffer from ADHD.

My wife and I would sit there together as the doctor would begin to ask Joshua a series of questions for a good forty-five minutes. The doctor and Joshua would have a nice conversation and the doctor would be taking notes during the examination.

My wife and I were amazed on how well Joshua would communicate with this doctor and answer all the questions honestly and intelligently. Joshua would maintain eye contact with the doctor, and for a child of this age, I could sense and feel that Joshua was truly gifted and a great communicator.

Joshua sat there for two hours and never once asked the doctor to get up and take a break. Joshua is famous for getting up within the first two minutes after we sit down at church to say he has to go to the bathroom. Joshua would use this as an excuse so that he could wander around the halls downstairs for ten minutes so that church would go by faster.

Joshua **was not** showing one sign of any hyperactivity and he just calmly sat there in his chair engaged in this conversation. After forty-five minutes of talking with Joshua, the doctor now turned his attention over to my wife Susanne and me. The doctor wanted more information from us concerning Joshua and his behavior at school and at home.

I think my wife and I were more nervous than Joshua, knowing we were up next and had to answer questions for the next forty-five minutes. We both gladly shared with the doctor all the shortcomings that Joshua had encountered in the past because we wanted him to have a full understanding of Joshua. We knew it was important for the doctor's evaluation.

After two hours, the doctor said that he did not believe that Joshua had ADHD and he was a normal young boy. Joshua knew full well that the actions that he took would lead to consequences. Joshua struggled with organization and understanding the importance of prioritizing things in his own mind.

My wife and I were relieved knowing that we would not have to put Joshua on medication. We knew that we could continue to work with him. We helped him work on improving certain organizational skill sets that would only help him do better in school and later in life. I know many adults who also struggle with organization and have difficulty prioritizing.

Life Lesson: *When your child struggles in school talk with him or her and find help.*

We all left the doctor's office feeling satisfied knowing that Joshua had work to do, but together we would be there offering him our love and support. We decided to keep him on the IEP at school. We knew the extra help from teachers, especially Mrs. Eddy in the learning center, would be very beneficial to Joshua.

At about four in the morning, I awoke with a revelation concerning my son Joshua. I had been thinking about him and was relieved that he did not have to take medication, but was concerned as to why he acted out in school and misbehaved at home. I wanted to know why he would fight my wife and me on everything we asked him to do. We were only trying to teach him about responsibility and things that would only benefit Joshua.

It all starts with the attitude that Joshua and all of us choose every morning when that alarm goes off. When that snooze or procrastination button tempts us, we have a choice. We can get up right away with a positive attitude, looking forward to our day, or we can be negative and start thinking about all the things that we do not want to do today.

I wanted to help Joshua stop all the procrastination and become more positive and I came up with the **If – Then** take action principle. **If** *you don't want to do something,* **Then** *do it right away*! This is a contradiction statement and designed to help you transform any negative thought or comment you make in your mind into a positive outcome.

If you think for a moment when you make a negative statement in your mind about something that you don't want to do, then you take the opposite approach that is a positive thought and action. Hopefully, you turn a negative into a positive.

You are contradicting your first thought and this process is designed for you to take action. The outcome will be a positive one and will benefit the individual. I am not suggesting that you use this method in any way that will lead you to have a negative outcome and harm yourself or health.

Life Lesson: *The choices that we make, lead to an action that we take, so let it be a positive outcome for goodness sake.*

The next day was Saturday and I sat Joshua down and we began to talk about all the things that he does not want to do. I calmly asked him to write down on a piece of paper all of the things that he did not want to do. I explained to him that he would awake daily and begin his day with a negative statement. I could not remember him ever starting his day saying something positive, especially when it came to all those things that kids his age don't really want to do like go to school, church, study and clean their room.

I explained to Joshua that we are able to actually choose our attitude towards something. If it is a positive thought, you embrace the task at hand, and performing it is not that bad. Joshua needed to appreciate and take gratification for completing a task like cleaning his room with a positive attitude and understand that it is a good outcome for him.

Life Lesson: *We can choose our attitude today so let's make it a positive one.*

We all really do not want to live in a messy home or room. We all feel better when it is clean and looks nice so use that as the outcome that you desire to motivate you to get it done. Stay positive and perform the duty with pride, knowing at the end you will feel good about it.

I explained to Joshua that the next time he woke up and said that he did not want to go to school, I wanted him to use the **If –then** take action principle. **If** *you don't want to do something,* **Then** *do it right away.* *This* statement would change his mindset. I asked him to write down on a piece of paper all the things that he really did not want to do and pick those tasks he would fight with his parents over, like not wanting to go to school.

Joshua embraced the idea and began to write down his first one, which was **If** *I don't want to go to school,* **Then** *do it right away.* The do it right away command is an action statement designed to help snap him out of the negative mindset. He would try to think about all the positive things that he actually did like about school. The positive things were spending time with his friends, gym, lunch, science, and sports.

After the upper half of his brain kicks in, which is where we do our reasoning, Joshua discovered that he had some fun at school and going there was not all bad. He began to realize all the positive things that occur and understood that the learning processes in the classrooms would benefit him and have positive outcomes for him later in life.

That is exactly what the **If-Then** action principle is designed to do, trigger the upper half of your brain to help you understand the situation and look at all the positive things surrounding it. The lower half of our brain is where all our fears and negative thoughts are housed. The lower half of our brain can consume us with fear and then self-doubt will settle in. Once you allow this half of your brain to control you and your day is negative.

Joshua was beginning to catch on but I could see that it was a little confusing. I had him write down ten **If – Then** take action statements. **If** *you don't want to do something,* **Then** *do it right away.* Joshua would apply them to all those things that he did not want to do. He would really understand it and try to apply the technique each day. He would try to find something positive from each of the situations that he always felt so negative about.

The first one he wrote was **If** *I don't want to take a shower* **then** *do it right away.* Joshua would stop procrastinating and just get in the bathroom and take the shower. He knew that keeping his body clean was both healthy and a positive outcome for him. Joshua grew tired of fighting mom and dad over this simple request went in and got it done.

The next one that Joshua wrote down was **If** *I don't want to do my chores* **then** *do them right away.* Joshua began to understand that doing his chores was helping him to appreciate hard work and he received an allowance for completing them. Joshua liked earning money because he enjoyed going to the mall with his big brother and buying video games, which was a positive outcome.

Life Lesson: *Save time and energy by doing the task right away.*

The next one that Joshua wrote down was **If** *I don't want to do my homework and study* **then** *just do it right away.* Joshua would come home from school and fight with his mom for an hour about getting his homework and studying done. He wanted to go downstairs and play his video games. The video games and fun time would become the positive outcome for Joshua and it helped to stop the procrastination. He stopped fighting with us, came home and got his homework done. Once the task was completed he could have fun and he gained an extra hour of fun time by not fighting with his mom.

Joshua wrote down all ten and I was very proud of him for completing this assignment because he began to get the idea. Joshua understood that he **could choose his attitude** and handle all of his life situations much differently in the future. Joshua grew tired of always being negative and became mentally stronger. He used this technique to help him try to remain positive while performing his duties and his behavior and grades improved.

I was having lunch the other day with a good friend of mine and he began to tell me a story about his nineteen-year-old son. He had been reminding his son for three months that he needed to get his car inspected. The son kept telling himself that he didn't want to go and get his car inspected.

The young adult, like so many of us, did not want to take the time and effort to drive to the local gas station and spend twenty-nine dollars to get the car inspected. The boy procrastinated and was not thinking about all the repercussions that could be in store for him if he was ever pulled over by a policeman.

A few days passed and the young adult was pulled over by a policeman. The policeman stopped him for not having a current inspection sticker on his car and while questioning him, noticed an open container of beer in the back seat. There was only a drop of beer left in the can and did not actually belong to this young adult because he did not drink alcohol. His friend left it in the car.

The policeman then proceeded to do his job and actually arrested this young man because he was only nineteen years old. Having an open container of beer was a crime. The young man was handcuffed and put into the back of the police car. The young man was so embarrassed he did not want to call his father, knowing his dad would probably be upset. If he only listened to his father and had the car inspected, this whole mess would have been avoided. The young man spent five hours in the local jail and was released on his own recognizance. He was asked to report to court the following week to answer to the charges that were filed against him.

The young man had his car towed and had no way to get home so he had no choice but to call his father for a ride home. His father showed up and during the ride home got all the details from his son. His father was not upset, considering his son had already been through enough while spending five hours in the local jail.

Life Lesson: *Don't delay the important things, especially concerning your car and safety. Stop the procrastination and lets getter done.*

His father was a little disappointed that his son did not call him earlier so that he could have been released from jail sooner. The father and son reported to court to answer to the charges the following week. The father helped explain everything to the judge and the charges were reduced. The son was given forty hours of community service and ordered to pay a **one thousand dollar fine.**

After my friend was done telling me all about the unfortunate circumstance that his son had to withstand, I decided to share with my friend some issues we were dealing with my son Josh. I told him about Joshua and all about the breakthrough we had with him using my new

If – then take action principle. **If** *you don't want to something,* **Then** *do it right away.*

I said **If** *you don't want to get your car inspected* **then** *do it right away.* If the young adult had used this as a way to motivate himself and change his negative mindset into something positive, then he would have experienced a more beneficial outcome. The young man chose to procrastinate and as each day went by, not following his father's advice, it was only a matter of time before he would get caught and the result would be a negative outcome.

The young man only had to pay twenty nine dollars to get the car inspected and maybe a half hour of his time to do the right thing and get it done right away. He now had to pay a one thousand dollar fine for court, spend forty hours painting the police department as community service and three hundred dollars to get his car out of the police impound yard. He also got arrested, spent five hours in the local jail and it all could have been avoided if he would have listened to his father and got the car inspected.

We all wake up every day with negative thoughts and tell ourselves that we don't want to do something. We are all human and it is simply the way we are. I am only asking all of you to try this new technique vigilantly to make sure you accomplish that task at some point the same day. Don't let your first negative thought shape your attitude today.

I love New Year's resolutions and the most popular one has to be exercising to lose weight. I am sure that there are many of you out there who wake up in the morning and have said that you don't want to exercise today. I say this all the time and how about you?

If *I don't want to exercise today* **Then** *do it right away.* Doctors tell us we need thirty minutes a day of exercise. Walking is a low impact popular way of getting it. I use this statement and force myself to find thirty minutes **every day walking**. It can be at your lunch hour at work or at eleven thirty that night. Spend the last thirty minutes of today walking up and down your stairs to accomplish this task today and end the day positive.

I use the **If-Then** take action statement to challenge me and change my mindset from a negative to a positive. I will not go to bed unless I accomplished that task today because I know if I quit one day it will be to easy too just keep quitting the next day. We are so busy running around working and taking care of our children that we must find thirty minutes a day to walk. Do it for yourself and your health so you are around to help others.

Life Lesson: *In life we don't always have to learn things the hard way to get them done.*

I want to thank Joshua for sharing with the whole world and me a few of the life issues that he had to deal with in his young life. I am confident that there are other children and adults who read this book who can learn and benefit from his story. They will also gain strength and come to realize that being positive and stop procrastinating will help them achieve their goals and succeed.

Joshua, you are a true inspiration and strong willed young man with a very bright future ahead of you. I think you will make one heck of a trial lawyer if you decide that is something you want to pursue, as you get older. Anyone who can communicate and respond quickly with intelligent answers to questions the way you do is destined to become a well-respected attorney.

Joshua understood and realized that he could choose his attitude every day. Any time that he begins to think negatively about any activity, like going to school, he will use the **If- Then** action statement to help change his mindset. Joshua also realized that his body language changed for the better as his outlook and mindset became more positive.

Joshua and all of you have the power in your own mind to change the way you may feel and think about a responsibility or activity. We can control our thoughts and I want all of you to feel confident that positive thinking is a simple task. Joshua has embraced change in his young life and I believe that all of you can do the same.

Joshua has improved his grades and his behavior at school after changing his mindset from a negative to a positive. All of his teachers have indicated that he is a completely different student and they are amazed with his quick turnaround. They told us that he looks and sounds much more confidant and is listening much better. They all want to know the name of the doctor who helped him out.

Joshua did not need a doctor and medication to help change his mindset. It was Joshua himself that became more focused. He accepted responsibility for his actions and started his day off with positive energy and not negative thoughts. Joshua chose to do this and had fun using the **If-Then** principle and applied them when he felt it necessary.

If you or your child have similar problems such as Joshua experienced, then follow the steps that we did as parents. We met with our school and asked them to test him for ADHD. Once we got their results and feedback, we met with our child's pediatrician.

We followed his recommendations to speak with a psychiatrist. Get all the expert opinions and understand that you and every child are different. The **If- Then** positive statement can work with everyone and we all agree that being positive is a good thing.

Joshua embraced the **If - then** action principle and understood that starting off each day with a negative thought did shape his attitude and he did not want to get into trouble anymore at school or at home. Joshua wanted to make the change and as his father I knew that there was a solution. Procrastination is always followed with a negative thought or statement and Joshua realized that he needed to stop that mindset and process before it would shape his whole outlook for that day.

My wife and I had tried everything before trying to help Joshua such as taking things away that he loved the most like video games, cell phone, sports, etc as a means to get him to take responsibility for his bad behavior and low grades. This would work but only for the short term. I knew we needed Joshua to want to make this mindset change so that long term he could grow as a person and accept the responsibility for his actions.

Communication with your child is the most important thing that I can recommend to all of you. I had to stop and listen to Joshua and get a better understanding on how he was really feeling about school. I had to change my approach while working and trying to help find a solution that will work best for Joshua. ***I had to stop yelling at him and telling him what he had to do.*** He is twelve years old and my approach towards him had to change from just a father and disciplinary to a person who will listen and talk calmly. We needed to work together and agree with a long-term solution to help him change his mindset from always being negative to become more positive. Joshua had to embrace and buy in to this **If-Then** action principle and use it as a guide to help himself.

As parents we know that every child is different and I learned much working with Joshua as we helped him find a solution that would work best for him. We have fun and from time to time he will revert back to his old self and indicate that he does not want to do something. He is only human like me and all of us. I will calmly say, **If** you don't want to do something and he will finish by saying **then** just do it right away and we both laugh. He will then just do it right away and stop the procrastination and get it done. Our relationship as father and son has grown stronger as I treat him more like an adult and not a child. Joshua has taught me much about being a better father and my need to listen.

I said it earlier and will say it again my youngest son Joshua is **brilliant** and a great communicator. He was blessed with a big kind heart and a personality that will light up any room that he walks into. He is a magnet and people are drawn to him with his kindness and good nature. He is not malicious and any trouble that he did get in school was very minor. We want him to understand that while growing up in your community your reputation and perception people may think of you is created by and controlled by you. I tell both Jacob and Joshua that you never do get a second chance to make a first impression. It is important to make sure all interaction with people is a positive one.

Life lesson: *Always remain positive and treat people the way you would like to be treated. Your character and reputation is based on your daily actions in life.*

Fifth Inning

Understanding the Importance of Being a Good Student Athlete

I wish somebody had told me the importance of being a good student athlete when I was in high school many years ago. I managed to get the good athlete part down which was a gift from God and came naturally, but failed at the most important part which was being a good student.

I find myself today telling my sons, Jacob and Joshua and all the kids I mentor, about the importance of being a good student athlete. I always say that if you love a particular sport then use that to motivate you to do well in school. The reason I say this is if you fail a subject, you cannot play the sport you love so much.

There is zero tolerance for failing in the classroom and your athletic career is the price you will pay for not passing a class. We need to pay attention and stop clowning around in school. We can all pass a class with some effort, and if you struggle ask the teacher for extra help. Be honest with the teacher and they along with your guidance counselor are a great resource helping you to get your grades back on track.

We need to apply as much practice to our schoolwork as we do getting ready to play any particular sport. Practicing your schoolwork means reading and studying. We must listen to our teachers when they lecture us about subjects that we know nothing about. It also means doing more then just the minimum to get by and we need to be competitive by winning good grades. Take pride in your schoolwork as much as you do with athletics.

If you are a competitive and passionate athlete, then apply that same effort you put forward on the athletic fields into the classroom. Being a good student takes more mental toughness than being a good baseball player because you may not like the subject that the teacher is trying to educate you on. In this situation only you can dig deep trying to concentrate and focus even more to motivate yourself to listen so that you can win a good grade and pass the class. This requires mental toughness to fight all those urges you maybe having as your mind wonders and you begin to daydream in class like I used too.

You may not be that interested in a particular subject but need to pass that class. I advise you to get excited about the class and study hard to pass the exams. This requires you to change your mindset and become more positive about school in general because it is the most important thing that you we all have to do as a youth. You have to go to class everyday and keep up with the daily workload so you stay on track and are keeping up with one topic before the teacher moves on to the next one. If you begin to fall behind on the daily and weekly assignments then you're setting yourself up for failure on the final exams at the end of the quarter.

Life Lesson: *Hit the books or you will not be allowed to hit the athletic fields and miss out on all the fun playing the sport that you love the most.*

In baseball, I found much success getting clutch hits in the bottom of the ninth inning, driving in winning runs for my team during our last at bats. I found out the hard way that you couldn't wait until the end of the quarter to study and try to pass a final exam when you did nothing to prepare for it the entire quarter.

I thought that I was that good in class and could pull off a good grade at the last minute, but when I got the exam back and it was below passing it was too late for me and I lost my privilege to play baseball. I think back to all the time I wasted not picking up the book and studying just a little every day and that would have made my life easier and I would have had a better chance to pass the final exam.

Life Lesson: *Doing a little work every day is easier then trying to get it all done the last minute.*

My oldest son Jacob is just as competitive in the classroom as he is on the athletic fields. My wife and I do not have to tell him everyday to get his homework done. He is self-motivating and takes it upon himself to do just that. Jacob is currently ranked number one in his class academically and it is because he is disciplined, focused and studies daily.

Jacob, and his friends Adam, Branden, Nick, Dan, Ryan, Kyle, Sean, Ricky, Daniel, Kristen, Kelsey, Marinna, Shannon, Kate, Leah, Kasie, Ashley, and Emily all think alike and have the same passion for school. They were all over my house one summer evening sitting outside on the deck by the fire talking. I went out to add a few more logs to the fire and happened to catch a little bit of the conversation.

I was inadvertently eavesdropping as I was adding the logs to the fire and was amazed to hear that they all were talking about the next school year and how excited they were looking forward to it. We were in the middle of the summer and I am sure the kids were talking about other stuff but this is a topic I never would have imagined they would be discussing now.

These kids are the top student athletes in their classes and they have discovered the importance of being a good student athlete. It is not surprising that these are the ones who are always listed when the highest honor role is distributed. They are setting high expectations for themselves and preparing for the future and are all successful.

They are all an inspiration to me and I learned a valuable lesson from them that night. School is cool and twenty-seven years ago when I went to high school these types of kids would probably be considered nerds for talking about school in the summer. I can attest to you that these kids are **definitely not nerds** and have so much more on the ball today than I had or any of my friends ever had back when I was in high school.

I consider them an **elite group of student athletes** because they are focused, mentally strong, positive, goal and results oriented. They are our leaders of tomorrow and know how to have fun, getting along with each other and aspiring to be the best that they can be. They are a great bunch of kids, and even though they are friends, they all compete with one another, both in the classroom and on the athletic fields, pushing and supporting one another to achieve greatness.

Life Lesson: *Treasure every minute of time you have together with friends in your school and are supportive to each other as you all find your place in this world.*

This elite group of student athletes understands that being a good student athlete requires time management, multitasking and great organizational skills. They are able to **juggle** all the activities that go on in school and on the athletic fields while maintaining top grades.

We all remember that expert juggler at the circus. He would be out there and he could juggle anything. He would juggle six bowling pins all at once with no problem, or nine baseballs very easily keeping them all up.

This elite group of student athletes mentioned is similar to the expert juggler at the circus because they are trying to juggle school activities and athletics. They have found a **balance** in their life and are able to juggle both of these and excel at a high level.

If we think of the elite student athletes as jugglers and assign a baseball to each activity that they are attempting, we can try and understand how they are able to keep them all up in the air. The first baseball represents their **schoolwork.** Imagine when they start juggling this first baseball.

If they only had to focus on juggling that one baseball, this group can now go from a 95 average to a 100. So let's toss them a second baseball, which will represent a **school sport** that they maybe participating in. They now are juggling two baseballs while trying to keep them both up in the air at the same time and maintaining top grades.

This now becomes a little bit harder for our elite group of student athletes as they try to juggle two baseballs at the same time. These **two baseballs represent schoolwork and athletics.** They are able to keep juggling both baseballs because they have excellent time management and organizational skills, along with the ability to prioritize their activities.

If we throw them a third baseball, which represents their **social life** and spending time with friends, now keeping up with juggling all three at the same time becomes even more difficult. This elite group of student athletes is doing just that and now they become more focused, making sure to prioritize. **They consider schoolwork to be number one, athletics number two and social life number three.**

The fun time with friends is important but they place that third on their list of things to do. When they all find that time to be together, it is an opportunity to unwind and enjoy the distraction from school and athletics.

Some other kids, including myself when I look back on high school, we would have prioritized those three activities much differently. For me it was athletics first, social life second and schoolwork third.

I now look back and understand why my grades suffered because school was not first on my list. I did not have good organization or time management skills. I definitely did not prioritize properly by placing school third on the list. I did not prepare myself well for the future and was heading down a path of self-destruction in high school.

If I look back to high school, I would fail as a juggler trying to keep these three baseballs up in the air all at once. I could easily maintain juggling one baseball, which is athletics, especially considering baseball was my favorite sport. I could probably handle throwing in that second baseball for my social life, but once you threw me that third baseball for schoolwork I would drop the ball.

Life Lesson: *We need to find a balance in life and prioritize our responsibilities.*

I did not prioritize my responsibilities in the correct order. I did not have the time management and organizational skills necessary to juggle all three activities as our **elite group of student athletes** are easily doing today.

If you are like me, then take a look at your activities and if schoolwork is not number one then you must make a change and place that at the top of your list. This is why the school will not allow you to play sports if you fail a class. They are trying to teach you to change your priorities and are asking you to focus more of your attention by putting the classroom first and not third on your list of things to do like I did as a knucklehead.

Let us throw a fourth ball at this elite group, which represents **employment**. Some of these kids also hold a part-time job working either as a referee, umpire, caddying, etc. I want you all to imagine them standing their juggling **four baseballs** right now trying to keep them all up in the air.

They are still juggling the first baseball that is *schoolwork*, the second baseball that is *athletics*, the third baseball that is a *social life* and now the fourth baseball that is *employment.* As you keep adding baseballs to your juggling, you may want to consider changing your priorities and the order of importance.

The fourth baseball, which is employment, may need to step in front and replace your third baseball social life and move down to the fourth position. We would all love to hang out with our friends more, but working may move up on that list of priorities because you need money to put gas in your car. You also need money so you can go out to the movies with your friends.

It is important for all of us to always continue to look at our responsibilities and make those necessary changes to your juggling order so that you are achieving your goals and still working hard by staying focused and keeping all four baseballs up in the air. We need to make sure that we have set them in the proper order with school at the top.

Life Lesson: *As you take on my responsibilities try not to overwhelm yourself and set realistic expectations.*

This elite group is now juggling four baseballs and it is getting much more difficult now for everyone, including this elite group of kids. If we remember to apply our three principles of **time management**, **prioritization** and **organizational skills** everyone can achieve this and keep juggling those baseballs.

Let us throw a **fifth baseball** at this elite group of student athletes. They are currently juggling four baseballs. Adding a fifth baseball, representing **family time**, is going to make anyone feel overwhelmed including this elite group. Imagine yourself standing their juggling five baseballs. They are **school, athletics, work, friends, and family**.

Life Lesson: *You need excellent time management skills to juggle many activities.*

We need to make sure that we have them in the correct order of importance. We already made one change when we added that fourth baseball and moved our friends down a spot because work was more important. Unfortunately we may have to consider moving our friends down another spot on the list considering that your family maybe more important then spending time with your friends. It is your choices on this order so think it over.

If your friends are wondering why you have been unable to spend as much time with them as you had in the past, let them know that you still enjoy their company and love hanging out but you have to get your grades up. Tell them you need more time to get schoolwork finished and your social life will have to take a back seat until you accomplish this.

If they are truly your friends then they will understand. If they don't understand, then you may need to start hanging out with kids who are the like the elite group of student athletes. You can juggle all five baseballs like this elite group, but may need to make sacrifices and changes. I never said that it was going to be easy.

I was fortunate enough to have a lot of friends in high school. I am still friendly with them today. After getting married, working full time, raising my family and juggling everything that I am responsible for, unfortunately they are my last baseball to juggle.

Don't let your friends put peer pressure on you that will only end up hurting you. I guarantee you one thing; if you stay in contact with just one friend after high school then you are like everyone else. I have been out of high school for twenty-seven years and after having so many friends, I really only talk and hang out with one.

If you are failing a class, then it is imperative that you take a hard look at how you're spending your time and make changes immediately. This is your life and in the end you will only end up getting hurt if you flunk out of school. Remember to think ahead ten years from now when you will be out in the real world working full time to support yourself and maybe your own family. Your education is important and it will help you achieve success in life.

In our economy, people with college degrees are having a tough time finding a good paying job. How do you think a high school drop out will compete with other people who earned a college degree? You need to understand that it is your life, so make sure you set your priorities straight and list them in the correct order that will catapult you to success.

Our elite group of student athletes is now **juggling five baseballs**. I think that is a lot for any person to have to juggle, including this elite group of student athletes. Take a moment and look at your life and all the activities that you are involved in and responsible for. Make sure you prioritize them from top to bottom and if you are failing school, then it is okay to take one or even two baseballs out of your juggling act and focus only on school because at the end of the day that really is most important.

Life lesson: *Be a leader and not a follower. It is your lives so make the right choice to benefit yourself and understand how it can be a positive affect in the long run.*

We all need to find a **balance in life**. We need to take on the responsibilities that we are comfortable with and that we can handle. We do not need to put any extra pressure on ourselves. If you can only juggle two baseballs, school and athletics, then stick to that plan. Everything else will have to wait and once you become more efficient at time management and organization, then try adding another baseball to your juggling act.

If you're like me and did not make the highest honor rolls in high school, do not get frustrated. We all want to strive for that top grade but try to remain realistic. If you are trying your best and studying, then feel good about the grade that you are getting. Remember the fourth C from chapter three. **Continued improvement** means that we all can improve, including getting better grades.

It is important that you are passing every class and making your schoolwork your top priority so that you can enjoy playing sports and other fun extra-curricular activities going on at your school.

These elite student athletes are over achievers and are great examples. You and I may be much different. If we only had to juggle one baseball for schoolwork, there is no guarantee that will put us on the highest honor roll. We are all built differently and have special gifts. Stay positive and continue to believe in yourself.

These elite groups of student athletes have built their own support group and all share common goals. Each of them is unique and special, like all teenagers, but together they have found the secret of success. It is a strong desire to be number one both in the classroom and on the athletic fields. They can count on each other for help and **I offer them all this next challenge.**

One day I hope each of them will use their knowledge and **mentor** someone less fortunate and become a **volunteer.** Juggling these two additional baseballs in anyone's life would be hard, but I believe in giving back to your community and sharing all the gifts that God has bestowed on you. I have come to know that there are two types of people in this world takers and givers. Takers are the ones who are always looking out for themselves and what's best for them and only them. Givers are those who are always trying to look out for others and helping to make somebody else's life bright and they sleep well at night. I consider myself to be a giver and ask that all of you try to understand the importance that your gifts and knowledge may help another so share them. God blessed me with skills and knowledge of the game of baseball and a positive motivational outlook on life. I am opening up my heart and exposing myself to all of you with all my personal mistakes and shortcomings in the effort to hopefully benefit you.

I have come a long way from high school and hopefully people will consider it to be a good one. I have grown as a person and as I took on more and more responsibility, I began to appreciate life and tried to enjoy all that life provided us. I never made the highest honor roll in high school but I would like to share with all of you the nine baseballs that I currently juggle as an adult. I will let you decide if you think that they are worthy of consideration for the highest honor role, if you were to grade me on these. I have found a balance in my life and wish all of you the same.

Life Lesson: *You will always remain friends, but as you get older accept that you will settle in life somewhere and other things will take priority.*

Here are the following nine baseballs that I juggle every day. As an adult, I am trying to keep them all up in the air at once. The first baseball that I juggle is **work**; I need to support my wife and two sons and provide them with shelter, food, clothing, etc., and it is expensive.

The second baseball that I juggle is **fathering**; I need to be here for Jacob and Joshua, supporting and guiding them to adulthood. I try to help them stay positive in all that they attempt to accomplish in their journey through life.

The third baseball that I juggle is being a good **husband**; my wife needs my love and support. I need to be there for her and give my time to listen as she works hard spending most of the time caring for our two sons, our home and me.

The fourth baseball that I juggle is **family**; I need to find time for my parents, brothers, sisters and their children. Your family is very important, as they will always support you.

The fifth baseball that I juggle is **exercising;** staying healthy by eating right and staying in shape both physically and mentally. It is impossible for anyone to juggle one baseball if they are laid out on their backs, out of shape and ill.

The sixth baseball that I juggle is **mentoring**; I share all my knowledge with other young adults and their parents who can benefit from it and writing this book demonstrates that.

The seventh baseball that I juggle is **volunteering**; as the president of Little League and a member of the Lions Club, I give my time to help my community.

The eighth baseball that I juggle is **coaching**; I coach both Jacob and Joshua in all the sports they play, along with other children in the community.

The ninth and final baseball that I presently juggle is **social life**; I do like to spend time with my friends golfing, bowling, and just hanging out, but unfortunately this one is last. I have decided that other responsibilities have to come first.

I try to be a good mentor and volunteer my time to any worthwhile cause in my community. God blessed me with the knowledge of baseball so in turn, I feel obligated and grateful to share all that knowledge with my sons and any other person that needs it.

As the president of Little League, I had the opportunity to share my knowledge with all the children who played in our program. If you have a special gift and knowledge in any area and know somebody who can benefit from that, then become a mentor and share it.

People do need a **mentor** and you can make a difference in the life of not only your child but also somebody else's child. We do not want you to waste the gift that God gave you so become a mentor and volunteering in your community is an opportunity for you to pay back what your community has given you over the years.

Life Lesson: *Over time you can learn to multi-task so never give up trying.*

While I was the president of Little League, my wife and I made sacrifices. The rules were that I could not coach a team because I had to remain neutral and make decisions that would benefit each child that played in our program.

I began to look at the larger picture, which was that I could build a stronger baseball program that would benefit everyone. If the overall baseball program were stronger, my sons who played in the program would benefit just as much as all the kids who wanted to play baseball.

This was an opportunity for me to give back even more to my community by serving the greater good of all the children and not just my sons. I have been teaching both Jacob and Joshua all about baseball since they were in diapers. I could continue to coach them at home and practice with them every day and that would never change. I would remain their private coach and help them to overcome their challenges.

As the president of the league, my duties took me all over town. I accepted the sacrifice of not being able to coach my sons but I was not prepared to miss watching them play. My wife would take over the cooking duties in our concession stand and together we both found it difficult to watch them play.

My wife was now making a big sacrifice and we both felt strongly about the success of the overall program and how much it benefited Jacob and Joshua. My wife and I would continue to support our two sons and all the kids that we came in contact with. My wife had a similar passion of helping children and together we decided to do this for eight years.

During my tenure as the president of the Little League, we accomplished much. We raised money and began to renovate all the ball fields by replacing the backstops, installing new score boards, laying new infield and outfield sod. Safety was the most important thing for all these kids and better fields would help them all develop.

I grew up playing on these same ball fields and they had lost their luster over time with no maintenance as the years passed by. My first goal was to get them back into tip-top shape for all the kids and spectators to enjoy. We restored pride to both the game of baseball and our community, as we would host other teams.

We celebrated fifty years of baseball a couple of years ago and to the delight of everyone we built a brand new regulation size Little League field. Besides the birth of Jacob and Joshua, my greatest accomplishment was making this field of dreams a reality. This new field would be here for future generations to enjoy. I am able to enjoy watching kids play baseball on a field where there used to be a vacant lot for fifty years. To me, this is truly a miracle and blessing from God. I thank everyone for helping me get it done for the kids.

Like most small towns, we all have to deal with politics. Although many people may have talked about building a new field prior to me becoming the president of the league, it never happened. It was a goal that I set. I would go out on a crusade meeting with every political committee our town had and fighting to make it a reality. I kept the kids at the heart of everything we did. I would present each committee with the same message. It was for all our children and they deserved the best our town can provide.

I hope all of you take a look at how many baseballs that you are presently trying to juggle. Prioritize them from most too least important. Keep in mind what is the best outcome for you in the end and work hard to achieve success

Life Lesson: *Plan your work and then work your plan.*

We would all love to juggle nine baseballs but take a look at where you are presently in your life. If you're in high school then that is too many baseballs to juggle. Be honest, set realistic expectations and limit yourself to those activities that you can juggle. If you are not in that elite group of student athletes don't worry.

I was not in that group either so take pride in what you can achieve and I always say if the grade is **A, B, or C** then you are in the top three. In the Olympics the **A** is a gold medal, the **B** is a silver medal and the **C** is a bronze medal. Stay positive; if you tried your best and earned a **C**, you passed and the school will allow you to play sports. Over time you can get better grades and there is nothing wrong with a **bronze medal**.

Try not to feel overwhelmed. If you do, then sit down and write all of the activities that you are trying to accomplish one by one. Begin to remove those less important activities from your juggling act. If you're feeling really stressed out and anxious, then you need to stop and take a deep breath. Keep everything in perspective and talk with your high school guidance counselor or parents. They are there to help you stay focused.

Together you can come up with a new strategy that will work best for you and your situation. You will never feel like you are all alone because with the aid of parents, the school or a mentor, ask for help and you will get it. I never would have gone to college if it were not for my high school guidance counselor Bob Perreault.

"Mr P" as we used to call him back then is the perfect example of what a mentor is and what a wonderful resource he was for me in my life. He never gave up on me and knew that for me to become successful in life I would need a college education. He took it upon himself to contact the head baseball coach at my college and then helped me to get into the school. I did graduate college on time, had a hall of fame collegiate career and met my wife during my four years in college.

Life Lesson: *Actions truly do speak louder then words become a mentor.*

Being a good student athlete also speaks volumes to your character, integrity, and core values that you are as a person. Perception that people may have on you comes from the actions that you take and the way that you act while your in school or working full time. Your principal, teachers, peers, and your boss will respect you for having the ability to juggle so many positive tasks. Somebody of importance is always watching so try to make a good impression.

I remember a major league baseball player who went to a charity golf tournament. He was being a good sport and signing autographs all day from the time that he showed up at eight am until the tournament was ending at six pm. He was out in the sun all day hot and tired and could not wait to get inside the clubhouse for a good meal and some much needed air condition to cool off.

He was walking in the clubhouse when a woman asked if he would sign an autograph for her child that was a big fan and considered him to be his idol. The athlete refused and felt like he did enough all day and was exhausted and skipped this last one and went inside to eat. This person happened to be a reporter and the next day the athlete got blasted in the newspapers and the headline read **top major league baseball player to good to sign an autograph for my child**. The major league baseball player spent ninety eight percent of his time that day doing all the right things and being very gracious to all and he let his guard down this two percent of his time that day.

It only takes two percent of our time to let our guard down and it will create a positive or negative perception of ourselves and we must always try to give that one hundred percent because you never know who is watching. This poor athlete had no chance to win in this argument once it hit the newspapers and it really was not fair for him to be judged that way considering all the good that he did that day. The people reading the newspaper did not have all the facts and at the end of the day it is the perception they all had towards him and it can all change in a second.

Life Lesson: *Remember the 98-2% rule and try not to let the two percent ruin all of the good that you do ninety eight percent of the time.*

Sixth Inning

Anxiety in Baseball and Life

While watching the Red Sox play on a Sunday afternoon, the announcer had been talking about a player for the other team who had been struggling with anxiety. He was an outfielder and great athlete. If you watched him on TV you could not tell that he was suffering from anything. This anxiety apparently became so much for this athlete he had to stop playing baseball for an entire season. He had been battling with anxiety for some time and being outside playing in front of thousands of people was something that he could not deal with. The player would later share his story with the public and he was not alone. Today we have several major leaguers who suffer from social anxiety disorder and these are players who are having a difficult time dealing with all the stress playing this game at such a high level.

These players each share one common characteristic and that is they are performing in front of thousands of people and if they fail they know everyone is watching. They also share the same symptoms when the anxiety attack occurs and those are rapid heart beating, sweaty palms, shortness of breath, weakness in the legs and feeling like your going to faint. The amount of money that these athletes command today also adds to the stress and anxiety of living up to those expectations. Some players who may be in a hitting slump or a pitcher who can't seem to find the strike zone share a common bond. When they go on the disabled list, otherwise known as the DL, it may be more than just a physical injury, it maybe all in their head.

Anxiety in the major leagues had been going on almost fifty years ago when hall of famers had to deal with the effects of some anxiety disorder. The only difference between those athletes and the present major leaguers is that the topic was not publicized back in the old days. Today, with the media in the locker rooms and the paparazzi following all these elite players around, they have no privacy anymore and have become public domain. These athletes make millions of dollars and some of them take everything in stride but for some others the whole experience can be downright terrifying.

The media does not care and all they want is a story. They want to know who is cheating on their spouse, and drinking to much alcohol. More stress is added to these athletes when the media follows them around, snapping photographs and camping out on their front lawns. The media would like to be there when they fail and show the whole world.

The media looks at the whole situation as a business and that maybe true but unfortunately this only adds more stress and anxiety to those certain athletes who are having difficulty handling the whole process. I am not interested in knowing about their personal life and those mistakes they made which is gossip. I would like to know more about the athlete who suffers from anxiety and how they are overcoming that challenge to succeed, so the rest of us can learn from them and apply those techniques to our lives.

Life Lesson: *Find peace in all that you do and remember you are only human.*

Athletes at all levels, not just the professional ones, deal with anxiety in some form. We all have experienced "butterflies" in our stomach before a big game. Athletes who are mentally strong can control their minds and thoughts and get all those butterflies to fly in the same direction. The athletes who are mentally strong and control all those butterflies in the stomach turn all that fear into triumph. They are able to conquer the fear or whatever is causing the anxiety and get out there and perform at the highest levels. These are the elite athletes who deliver that winning hit in the bottom of the ninth.

I began to wonder about all those athletes who got caught taking steroids. Major league baseball now has a time frame associated with steroid use and they called it the *"steroid era."* I am not an expert on anxiety or steroids but have heard that steroids can make your body physically and mentally stronger. **I never took them and neither should you.**

Obviously, most of the athletes who took steroids to get stronger hit more home runs. These athletes went from just being average to elite and turned their baseball careers into multi-million dollar contracts. Everyone benefited from the steroid era. Players made millions of dollars as the owners made billions. I think for some players taking steroids also made them feel invincible and mentally stronger. It gave them confidence and helped make them more capable of hitting those home runs to win games and championships for their respective teams. I do not believe you need steroids to make you mentally or physically stronger.

I believe that these athletes have hurt the game and disrespected the game of baseball. The game is bigger than all of them and the integrity of the game must outweigh the financial gain of a certain few. These athletes have also put their health at risk because of all the many side effects steroids have on the body. Did stress and anxiety have anything to do with some of these athletes making that decision to participate and take steroids? Did the steroids help these athletes overcome the stress and anxiety while performing out on the field in front of thousands of people and millions more watching on TV? We may never know if there is that correlation between anxiety in some major league baseball players and steroid use to help cope with all the stress. I believe that for some of them they might have found relief as the body and mind became more physically and physiologically stronger. I also believe that steroid use is not the solution.

If anyone would like to improve their game and get stronger then you have put the extra time in the gym lifting weights. I remember my first year in college and as a skinny freshman playing at the college level, all my fly balls would end up being caught on the warning track. My teammates called this having warning track power because I was not strong enough to hit the ball out of the park and over the fence. At the time, my captain took me under his wing and in the off-season we began to work out together lifting weights. We did it the old fashion way. We worked out four times per week increasing the strength in my chest, legs and arms without using steroids. I felt stronger physically and mentally and over the next three years began hitting more and more home runs.

Life Lesson: *Sometimes doing things the hard way is better for you in the long run.*

On Labor Day 9/2/2002, it was my day off from work and I decided to visit our local mall. I got to the mall early and entered an elevator on ground floor level C that was located in the parking garage. I rode that elevator up three floors to level three.

At level three, the elevator stopped and the doors began to open. I was standing in front of the elevator doors as they opened. I noticed that they only opened about three-quarters of the way and then began to close. Without hesitation, I leaped through the opening thinking that I could exit the elevator.

This was a mistake because the elevator doors were closing much more quickly than I first thought. The doors struck me on my right shoulder and the safety mechanism failed as the door continued to close and they would not stop. The elevator doors began crushing my upper torso and I had to twist my body and step back into the elevator. I did not have an opportunity to exit the car. The only choice left was to turn my body and return to the car because the doors just would not stop closing. I got my whole body back into the car and as I tried to pull my right leg in before the doors closed completely, it was trapped.

My whole body was now back in the elevator except my right knee which now was pinned between the elevator doors. The doors were still trying to close and they began crushing my right knee. Here I am standing on one leg in the elevator car and the bottom half of my right leg is now sticking out between the elevator doors.

I was trapped and screaming and in lots of pain as the elevator doors kept trying to close all the way. I was able to reach over and with my left hand pushed the emergency service button. A person got on the phone and I was screaming about my situation. They were sending mall security to the scene.

A woman happened to be walking past the elevator and heard my screams. She stopped and tried to open the doors from the outside as I tried doing the same from the inside. We had no luck and the elevator doors simply would not budge.

I pushed the emergency button a second time because several minutes had passed and mall security still had not arrived. After a couple of minutes nobody showed up at the scene. Smoke was now coming up from below the elevator car. The doors had been trying to close and since my leg was trapped, they could not close and the gears were grinding which created smoke in the car.

I began to feel lightheaded and started thinking "If somebody pushed the button on the first floor trying to use this elevator, would the car go back down and chop off my leg?" I was in a very bad situation because if somebody tried to use this elevator I could not move my leg because it was still trapped. I felt like I had lost all control of the situation and I was helpless. My fate and health were in God's hands.

Life Lesson: *Always being aware of your surroundings and don't assume you are invincible, whether you are taking an elevator, walking down the street or driving a car.*

I pushed the emergency button a third time and finally mall security showed up on the scene. It took them twenty minutes to get here after my first call. They thought I was stuck in the car and did not realize that my leg was trapped between the doors. They had a key that could shut down the operation of the elevator but it still would not open the doors.

I felt relieved knowing that nobody else could push a button on the lower floors and this elevator car could not move. Mall security tried to pry open the doors from the outside to free my leg but they were unsuccessful. Mall security had to call the fire department because they had the only key that would open the elevator doors. I had to wait another fifteen minutes for them to show up.

There were eight firefighters who showed up. They all thought I was trapped in the elevator car, just like mall security thought. They had no idea that my leg was trapped between the doors. The firefighters all grabbed the door and told me that they would try to pry it open slightly for me and force my leg back into the car. They would have to use all their might to move those doors just enough so that I could pull my leg back inside. It worked and as my leg was released, the car doors slammed shut and luckily all the firefighters moved their hands out of the way or they would have been crushed.

I was now completely inside the elevator car. The firefighters then used the key to open the doors that were now completely shut. I was finally rescued from the elevator car and was very lucky that I did not lose my leg. I was rushed to the hospital and diagnosed with a fractured right patella and was placed in a cast. The pressure from those elevator doors had cracked my kneecap in half and it was very painful. I would have to stay in the cast for two months and then undergo physical therapy.

After about six months of physical therapy, I was able to get around 90 percent of the mobility back in that right knee. To this day, it is still very weak and has not fully recovered. I feel very lucky, especially considering the fact it could have been much worse.

I could have lost the leg if somebody who was trying to use the elevator had pushed the button. It was pure luck that the mall was not busy that day and nobody needed to use that particular elevator. Although my leg began to heal, I began to deal with nightmares concerning the accident.

Life Lesson: *Any traumatic event can cause both physical and mental stress to you.*

I began to start thinking about all those things that could have gone wrong. I would wake up because of nightmares. I would be sweating, thinking about my leg being chopped off, or being killed in the accident. Although my body had begun to heal physically from this ordeal, I began to experience mental images that were terrifying.

After six months, I finally returned to work and had to visit a client one day. He was an attorney and located on the sixth floor. As I approached the elevator, I almost passed out. I had a flashback to my accident and could not get up the strength to get on the elevator that day. I had shortness of breath, began to sweat, my heart was racing, and my legs felt like jelly and was weak. I had to sit down and it was the first time in my life I ever experienced any feelings like that. I had no idea what was happening to me and I thought that somebody had poisoned my coffee. I actually felt like I was going to die, it was that bad.

I went in the bathroom on the first floor and poured water over my face as I tried to regain my composure. After ten minutes, I began to feel better and I approached the elevator a second time attempting to get upstairs. The symptoms came back once I approached the elevator and then I knew something was not right. I was terrified about the thought of getting back in an elevator. I took the stairs and finished my work for that day.

I made an appointment with my doctor and explained to him everything that I was feeling that day. He asked me to share with him how I was feeling during the six months after the accident. I told him that I was having nightmares, having difficulty eating, and I lost forty pounds in three months. I told him that I felt claustrophobic and felt like I was going to choke on my food. The doctor was concerned because I was not eating properly and had rapid weight loss.

The doctor had diagnosed me with post-traumatic stress disorder. He explained that the accident had such a traumatic affect on me both physically and mentally. The broken bones in the body would heal over time, but such a traumatic accident caused mental stress and anxiety.

I now knew what it felt like for some of those major league baseball players who had been dealing with anxiety. The ballplayers were dealing with a social anxiety disorder and mine was a post-traumatic anxiety disorder. The baseball players would have panic attacks at the ballpark while trying to perform in front of thousands of people. I had one while I attempted to ride an elevator for the first time after my accident. We shared similar symptoms with two different types of anxiety.

Life Lesson: *We are all human and any day a traumatic event can change our life.*

I had experienced those same symptoms as the major league baseball players and they are scary. You do feel like you are going to faint, your heart is racing; you have sweaty palms, shortness of breath and weak legs that feel like jelly. I basically felt like I was going to die. I also dealt with claustrophobia because being trapped in that elevator for an hour with no way out placed a lot of stress and strain on my mind and body. It is amazing the power our mind has over the body.

The nightmares that I had been experiencing began to take a toll on my mind and thus affected my eating and sleeping habits. I did not want to ride an elevator again and with good reason. I figured that I would simply avoid them and everything would be fine.

I read a lot about anxiety and for the first time I realized that if you fear something and try to avoid it like I had been with the elevator, it leads to other issues for your body. In my case it affected my eating. I literally felt like I was going to choke every time I ate food. I would have to line up five glasses of water and after taking each bite; I would drink a whole glass of water.

This is the power that your mind has over you and once you lose control of your thinking. It ends up affecting your body. I lost control over my thoughts and could not reason with myself and get past it so dealing with a simple task like eating became a nightmare.

We all agree that the two most important things are body's needs are food and sleep. I felt claustrophobic in my own body. In my mind, even eating yogurt was difficult. Yogurt is like drinking a milkshake but for me it was scary. That is why, I lost forty pounds in such a short amount of time as the anxiety began to control my thought processes and me.

My doctor recommended that I talk with a psychologist and work out these issues. It was weird for me because I was really not comfortable talking about my fears and concerns. I had no choice because my weight loss was a major medical concern and I had to get myself back to a normal weight and regain control of my situation. I felt embarrassed about this whole ordeal but understood it was a terrible accident and just had to make the best of it. I had no control over the accident and needed help to get control of my mind.

I visited with a psychologist for twelve one-hour sessions and it was the best thing that I ever did. I was able to explain to her all about the accident and my feelings afterwards. She listened and then educated me all about anxiety and all the different types that people experience. Anxiety has many different types of diagnoses but in the end, I reached this conclusion. It is up to me to control my thoughts and try to reason with the negative and stressful images that concerned me.

Life Lesson: *There is nothing to be ashamed about talking to a professional especially after any traumatic accidents, the loss of a loved one, or stress in your life.*

The doctor explained to me that we have two halves of our brain. The top half is where we all have the ability to reason during a situation or thought. The bottom half is where we house all our fears and is in charge of our most primal instincts. I needed to get the top half of my brain to start reasoning and process my fear of eating, so that I could regain control of my situation.

The bottom half of my brain began to take control over my entire thought process and it was happening at a subconscious level due to the trauma of my accident. I had become so afraid of elevators and thinking about all the really bad things that could have gone wrong that day, but did not, and I released what I consider to be this monster they call anxiety from the bottom half of my brain.

This monster that I created in my mind was out and only I could tame it and return it back to a place I felt that I had control. I needed to activate and stimulate the top half of my brain and regain control of my thoughts and actions. I needed to get the top half of my brain to reason, and turn these negative thoughts into a positive one. I needed to remind myself that I was fine and to breathe normally. Over time, these symptoms may come but I have realized that they will pass and I will be fine. You can do the same and realize that you are not alone.

It all goes back to what I wrote about earlier in this book and how we can truly choose our attitude. We can either allow negative thoughts to control us or we can take control and become positive. I had to be vigilant because, I had to take on the anxiety that, I created in my mind and regain control of my life and get back into the game of living.

Any traumatic event can be the trigger and be the cause of anxiety. The doctor told me that one in every four people deals with some form of anxiety, or they know somebody that does, and I believe it. I never thought that anxiety would ever affect me and I never planned on getting my leg trapped between two elevator doors. It was a horrible accident and many of you have been in one yourself or know somebody that has. Together we can make it better and I hope you find the strength to do just that.

If you watch the evening news and listen to all the horrible tragic events that are happening around the world every day, it is easy to understand why one in four have anxiety. Our troops come home from serving their country and deal with post-traumatic stress disorder frequently.

We all hear about our troops who struggle when they come home, trying to adjust back into society and trying to get back into a normal routine. I now know how difficult that is for them because if you suffer from anxiety the symptoms are similar. It maybe different events in our life that brought on the anxiety but in the end we all seem to feel the same way. I have found that I have suffered the same symptoms but they have it worse than me because they may have lost a limb or have seen a friend die in battle.

After the events of 911, people who watched those events on television ended up dealing with anxiety. Anyone who has ever been on an airplane can relate to what those people must have had to endure, as they looked out the windows, and saw those buildings so close knowing something was terribly wrong. They knew the plane was going down and their lives were over. They were trapped on the plane and it was out of their control.

That is how I felt being trapped in between those elevator doors and at the mercy of God. I had no place to go and with those elevator doors clutching onto my leg it was all out of my control. I looked around that stainless steel elevator car and to me it felt like a coffin. It is no wonder that I became claustrophobic from that traumatic event.

After twelve sessions with the doctor, I was taught about using visualization techniques to help me relax and reason whenever I had an anxiety or panic attack. I learned that those symptoms would occur from time to time, they would peak and then return too normal. I just had to be patient for ten minutes and let the symptoms work their way through my body. I would focus on trying to take deep breaths and visualize myself being someplace fun.

I used to visualize being at the beach on a warm summer day listening to the birds chirping and the waves crashing into the surf. **"*At the beach, watching four sea gulls, sitting side- by- side staring into the ocean*"** became a very peaceful thought for me and it helped me to deal with the panic attack much easier. I would have to take my mind to the beach and pretend that I am really there with all the sounds and smells of the beach. I would repeat the above quote ten times while having an anxiety attack to stimulate and activate the top half of my brain and it became a positive distraction to snap me out of it.

I would become a master of my thoughts and regain control of my life. I would have to deal with my fear of elevators, and eating. I could not let my fear control me any longer. I had to start riding elevators once again and that thought was terrifying but using the visualization technique and repeating the above quote ten times did help me get control while a panic attack occurred.

I went to a new hotel near my house and my wife and kids were in the car. They knew all about my fear of elevators and none of them could blame me. They also understood that I had to take this fear on and get myself back in the elevator, if I would ever truly be able to regain control of my life again.

Life Lesson: *If you fall off that horse pick yourself up and dust yourself off and get right back on it.*

I got out of my car and walked up to that elevator and pushed the button. I began to feel my heart race, my palms sweat and my legs felt weak. I visualized myself at the beach and repeated the quote ten times, **"At the beach, watching four sea gulls, sitting side-by-side staring into the ocean"** it would help to remind myself that I was okay. The doors opened up and I walked right in and pressed the button for the third floor. The doors closed completely and I had to wait a few minutes for the car to travel up and the doors to open. Those minutes felt like days, but the car stopped and I got off on the third floor. I felt great my anxiety symptoms started but went away. I had accomplished something that we all take for granted every day like riding elevators but I had survived. It was a big moment for my recovery and I would get stronger and stronger the more that I did it.

Riding an elevator is a simple task and you are all wondering, "What is the big deal?" After all that I endured, this was a big deal to me and I had just taken a major step forward in gaining control of my life again. I used the visualization techniques the doctor taught me and allowed the top half of my brain to control the bottom half, and I completed a simple task. I spent the next four weeks conquering my fear by riding elevators. The more I did it, the more comfortable I felt and my eating habits returned too normal. I believe that you can accomplish the same and I hope you find a solution.

Life Lesson: *Don't let any fear control your life, work to conquer the fear and move on*

A person's age has nothing to do with anxiety. We have learned about major league baseball players who deal with the affects of anxiety and you just read about the traumatic event that caused me to deal with anxiety. It can happen to any of us and if it does, try to use the visualization technique that I use to make it better.

A child awakes in the middle of the evening screaming, sweating, and fearful as the parents run to their room to console and comfort the child. The parents ask the child to explain what is bothering them. The parents inquire if the child had a nightmare. The child says that there is a boogeyman underneath the bed. The parents try to reassure the child that there is no such thing and they ask the child to look underneath the bed with them to prove the point. The child does find some comfort and begins to calm down but would like them to stay in the room with them all night because they have just experienced a traumatic event. The parents kindly refuse because they want the child to understand that there is no such thing as a boogeyman and they don't want to form a bad habit of sleeping with the child every night.

Has the Childs ***imagination*** just run away from them? Or is it a form of anxiety and panic attack from the nightmare. The child will still have that fear or thought in their mind after the parents leave the room and now would like the light to always stay on hoping that will solve the problem. The child will need to somehow work out all of this in their young mind. That is an awful lot for a young child who maybe five, six, or seven years old to accomplish. How does a parent try to explain to a young child about the two halves of their brain? How does a parent try to help the child to help itself activate and stimulate the top half of their brain to reason with the negative thought of no such thing as a boogeyman, which is a fear that arose from the bottom half of their brain?

My point is once the fear is unleashed in our mind something that maybe trivial to you because you are lucky to have never experienced the effects of a panic attack are devastating to the other person regardless of their age. We can help with some basic knowledge of the brain and how strong our negative thoughts can be in controlling our body. I believe that you can try to educate the child more as you do console and comfort them during this ordeal. I believe that it will make them mentally stronger and it is important for them to try to work these things out for themselves in the long run.

I recommend that if you suffer from anxiety, seek medical attention and get expert advice from your doctor. In the end it is up to you conquer the anxiety and regain control of your life. You need to get the top half of the brain to reason and gain control. The visualization technique is designed to distract your thoughts and snap you out of it.

I believe that all of you can regain control of your life and understand the power our minds have on the body. Your mind can control your body language and mood swings. It can control your eating and sleeping habits. Traumatic events may be the trigger that will release that monster the doctors all call anxiety.

I have a friend who asked me to talk with their ten-year old daughter. Her parents told her about my accident and we shared similar symptoms of anxiety. I am not a doctor, but I know my friends very well. Together with her parents, I shared my story with her.

She felt better knowing that she was not alone with these feelings. She looked at me and could not believe that somebody so confident and strong had once dealt with those symptoms. I told her that she was not alone and other kids in her school probably have experienced the same symptoms of anxiety and nobody could detect it is happening.

These are feelings that we all may have to deal with at some point in our life and for her it started at the age of ten. She was trying out for the cheerleading team and felt anxious about not making the team. She thought that maybe some of the other girls would not think that she is pretty or good enough. We all faced our own insecurities at some point in our lives. I did not judge her but took the time to listen and remind her that it is okay to feel that way, but do not let those negative thoughts consume her. She was also having difficulty sleeping and eating, worrying about these cheerleading tryouts.

I bought her a pair of big fluffy **happy feet** slippers. We talked about using visualization techniques and I told her all about mine at the beach.

I told her anytime she was home and felt anxiety symptoms occurring, she was to put the happy feet slippers on and walk up and down her stairs ten times using the visualization technique. She began to use this simple procedure and it worked for her. By walking up and down the stairs, she was using energy burning off those symptoms and she began to control her thought patterns. I told her every time the symptoms occurred they would peak and go away. She realized that everything was fine and over time each episode would make her stronger and stronger because in the end she was always fine.

Life Lesson: *Whatever does not kill you does make you stronger.*

If a ten-year old girl and I can overcome these anxiety symptoms then I believe that all of you can do the same. I know that everyone's situation is different, and certain events may have caused you to feel this way. Keep trying to regain control of your life but it is up to you to make that happen. I believe that you can do it and I have faith that you will find a way to tame that monster they call anxiety. Life is too short and you need to stimulate the top half of your brain and take back control of your thoughts.

It was not easy for me to share with the whole world how I felt after my horrible elevator accident and it is quite embarrassing. I felt it was important because maybe my story would help all of you. You are not alone and I have met many people who struggle with anxiety and after all sharing the same symptoms, I found it helpful to talk about it.

I have a high tolerance for pain and being an athlete I have dealt with many injuries. The anxiety symptoms are completely different and controlled me for a short period in my life. It was worse then any physical injury I ever had. I finally tamed that monster and have grown mentally strong from it.

I hope all of you find peace and are able to conquer your anxiety, so that you can go on and enjoy your life to the fullest. It is fine to meet and talk with a psychologist because this is their area of expertise. Don't feel embarrassed and remember that people who look at you daily have no idea you may be dealing with anxiety. We believe everyone around us can see what is going on in our lives, but that is not true. We just feel that way. Gain control of your thoughts and get back in the game of life and win.

Remember those major league baseball players who struggled with anxiety? They had the courage to get out on the ball field and perform in front of thousands of people. They were dealing with anxiety and confronted it head on. They let go of the anxiety and performed to the best of their ability.

We cannot let the bottom half of our brain where all the fear and self doubt live control our lives anymore. You must fight to regain control of your thought patterns and tame that monster they call anxiety. You do have the inner strength to make this happen and must believe in yourself and develop techniques that will help you get past the symptoms.

I hope that both my son's Jacob and Joshua never have to deal with these symptoms but if they do they now can think of me and know that they can gain control of this and they will be fine. It is not easy for me to write about such a personal traumatic event that happened to me in my life. I felt compelled to share it with all of you knowing it may touch somebody and hopefully offer up inspiration so that they can gain control of their life once again. I have become much stronger mentally from this traumatic accident and know that you can do the same. Life is not easy and we all feel overwhelmed sometimes so take it one-day at a time, put your trust and faith in God as you continue your journey to happiness.

I also learned that people who do suffer from anxiety are very intelligent. They are able to multitask and have great organizational skills. They have an active brain, which is constantly working as they try to come to grips with their fear and gain control of their life. These are characteristics that you should draw strength from and use to help keep you positive. There is always something positive that we can take from our own experiences and I want you all to find those and use them to help you in your efforts to fight that monster we call anxiety. Share your story with somebody that you trust and you will find out that you are not alone. I hope you will gain strength from my story.

Life Lesson: *Life is a journey so enjoy the ride and try not to take things so seriously.*

Seventh Inning

Health is Wealth

As a kid growing up, I always thought that I was invincible. I never thought that anything bad would happen to me. In high school my friends and I would begin to experiment with drinking beer. One of my good friends would host a sleepover party almost every Friday night and we would become known as the weekend warriors.

My friends and I would go to the local liquor store and we would somehow manage to get some person of legal age to buy beer for us. It was wrong for that person to buy beer for underage kids, but back then we all thought that it was cool and we wanted to act like adults. My friends and I were also wrong for asking this adult to do something illegal like purchase the beer. Participating in underage drinking is dangerous to any teenager, including my friends and me. Our bodies are not ready to begin consuming beer or any alcohol in high school.

As I look back on those high school days, we were young and dumb when it came to drinking. It would seem that at every sleepover party the ten of us would drink to much beer and we all learned a tough lesson that excessive drinking is dangerous for all age's especially underage kids. I learned that if you consume more then five alcoholic drinks in one day it is considered binge drinking. Binge drinking is unhealthy for your body.

Lenny Silva

Life Lesson: *Be a leader and not a follower; underage drinking is wrong.*

I kept reminding myself the day after that I would never engage in this behavior again. That would only last a week and when next Friday night rolled around, I was back at the party with my ten closest friends. I would repeat the same mistake over and over again and drink excessively right along side with my friends.

At the time, my friends and I did not have our licenses. This was a great thing because we would stay put at my friend's house and drunk driving is the most dangerous and irresponsible thing that any person of any age can engage in. All that would change as we headed into our senior year of high school.

My friends and I would continue to get together for our regular Friday night party from our freshman year through our senior year in high school. One night we decided to leave our regular Friday night party and go to another party that was being held up the street. I sat up front in the passenger's seat of the car along side two other friends one in the middle and the other who was driving. We all had been drinking prior to getting in the car. We were driving down this dark winding road and going too fast as my friend was navigating the car around these sharp turns. I had my passenger's side door window wide open because it was a hot humid night. I heard a voice in my head instructing me to roll up my window. I just had a terrible feeling that something bad was going to happen.

We were now approaching the sharpest S turn when my friend lost control of the car and we began to slide all over the road. We ended up driving into the side of the road, which was sloped, and the car went airborne like something you would see in a movie. The car rotated around once in the air, as we rolled over and landed on the passenger's side of the car.

The car had rested on its right side and rested between two huge oak trees. My two friends would end up sliding directly on top of me. Imagine those two friends and I were all pressed up against that window that I just recently closed. They were all piled up on top of me and we were trapped.

Nine Innings

Life Lesson: *If you have just one alcoholic beverage call for a ride home or take a cab.*

It was pitch black in the woods and we could still hear the engine running as the tires were still spinning, because the car landed on its side. My friend reached over and turned off the ignition to stop the car.

One friend stood up and stepped on our other friend and me. I was on the bottom of this pile as he tried to push open the driver's side door so we all could climb out of the car. We all were very scared not knowing if the car would blow up and catch on fire. We were trapped inside the car for several minutes, which felt like hours.

My friend was a big strong kid and using our bodies as leverage, he had the strength to push open the driver's side door. The weight of the door was too heavy to stay open by itself and it closed, forcing him and all of us back into the car once again.

We all forgot that the car was not sitting on all four tires but actually on its side so it was impossible for the door to stay open by itself. My friend tried it once again and this time he would push open the driver's side door and he had to climb out that side door and hold it open allowing us to follow one by one as we exit the vehicle.

We were all very scared and I kept thinking about one thing. I thought I had an angel with me that night because some voice instructed me to close the window. Closing the window was the only thing that kept my friends and especially me sitting right there inside the car as we crashed and rolled over in the woods. If the window had stayed open, my entire body would have been thrown out of the car and I would have been easily killed. Chances are, the car would have ended up resting on top of my body.

We were all very lucky that night and thankfully all three of us walked away from the accident with minor cuts and bruises. The police showed up at the accident and had to question my friend who was the driver. The accident had terrified all three of us so much we actually sobered up within minutes.

Life Lesson: *Never get in a car with anyone who has been drinking and never drive drunk.*

My friend was very lucky that he got off with a warning and did not lose his license for this accident. The police could smell beer on his breath but with no alcohol found inside the car, they had no proof that we had been drinking. The drunken driving laws back in 1983 were not as strict as they are today.

That same night two of our other friends also got into a car accident while they were on their way to this second party. They went off the road and hit a tree and both got rushed to the hospital. One of my friends had to stay for a week with a serious injury and they were also very lucky to survive that accident.

Life Lesson: *Don't drive drunk or let a friend drive drunk take their keys and call a cab or a parent for a ride home.*

Our graduating class of 1983 could have easily lost five classmates that night between the two car accidents. I could have been one of them and although I was not driving drunk, I got into a car with a friend who was. We were all acting stupid and irresponsible because we allowed ourselves to get into a dangerous situation. We never spoke up and took the keys away from our friends who were not in any condition to drive. I was not in any condition to drive either and we all should have just stayed at my friend's house the way we did before we got our licenses. The other five friends that we hung out with were smart, as they decided to stay at the first party and not get into any car.

The five of us who left that party that night and got into cars to go to the next party were all stupid, including myself. We made a bad decision that could have been life changing to all. Even though we were only kids and seniors in high school, we should have made a smarter decision and took ten seconds to think before we acted.

We all think that we are bullet proof and nothing bad is going to happen to us. Most of my friends and I felt that way. We did not consider the safety of the public and we were all selfish and inconsiderate of others. I learned a valuable lesson from the accident and for the rest of my senior year I began to make better decisions. I was getting older and trying to act more responsibly, especially considering that I was driving now. I did not want to lose my license and I scared my parents that night.

My parents knew that I was very lucky and they had worked so hard protecting me while I was growing up. They did not want to lose me now since I was almost finished with my last year of high school. I received a punishment from my parents for just being in the car and participating in underage drinking. It was a punishment that I welcomed and I learned from that mistake.

I was happy that I had an angel watching over my friends and me that night. It could have been much worse for our community and us. The community would have been devastated to lose five high school seniors in one night. I began to avoid the Friday night party for the rest of that year. I decided to look for another part time job.

While in high school I earned money as a baby sitter. I would babysit for two young boys every Friday night and became very close with them. I knew the parents well and twice a month, I watched the two boys while the parents went out. It was a great job for me. The boys were great kids and great athletes in town and I would check in with them, from time to time after I graduated high school. To the delight of my parents, I graduated high school and had survived all those Friday night parties with my friends. I was off to college and ready to begin a whole new chapter in my life.

My Friday night partying high school friends and I would all separate and head off into different directions when we went to college. We lost contact with each other as we all settled into the college experience and made new friends. We would get together once a year at the annual high school football game each Thanksgiving.

My four years in college were a blast. I made the college baseball team and had ten new friends to hang out with. We would always eat lunch together and as the best baseball team in the state we were a close-knit group. We would begin a whole new tradition of partying.

In college they have keg parties and we, as a group, did not miss many. We would all be considered regulars at the keg party scene in college and we would take binge drinking to a new level. I was older now and you would think that I should have learned my lesson in high school and stopped following the crowd.

I was in college now and along with my new friends, I wanted to experience everything. I was having fun playing baseball during the day, studying and hitting the keg party scene at night with my friends.

My new group of ten college friends and I all had the same things in common, playing baseball, girls, and drinking beer. We were all having a blast and enjoying the college experience. We were all considered binge drinkers while in high school and now once again, I was repeating those same mistakes again but now in college.

We would go to the keg parties and no one could stop after drinking two beers. My parents would always say, "*Everything in moderation*" but when we all got together it was next to impossible to have just two beers.

I knew that binge drinking **was not** the right thing to do but again I felt like I was invincible and nothing bad was going to happen to me. I kept drinking right along with my new college friends. We all drank too much and never took into consideration the damage it would have on our bodies.

Life Lesson: *If you can't have just one beer then just have* **NONE**.

I graduated college in 1987 in four years with a Bachelor's degree in Science and felt like I survived another four years of drinking. I had a Hall of Fame college baseball career, earned a college degree, and met the woman of my dreams. My life was great and even though I blew an opportunity to play professional baseball my future looked bright.

I returned home after college and received a phone call from my sister concerning the two boys that I used to baby-sit while I was in high school. One night the younger of those two boys had turned twenty-one-years old. His older brother decided that they would go out clubbing to celebrate. They would spend a nice night out together.

They were leaving a bar and the younger boy decided that he would drive home. The older brother sat in the passenger's seat and on their way home they got into an accident. They had gone off the road and smashed into a concrete wall and the car was completely crushed. The younger brother died instantly at the scene of the accident and the older brother would spend months in the hospital while his broken bones were healing. When I received that phone call and heard about this tragedy I was heartbroken.

The two young boys were very close to me and I considered them like my brothers. They were like family to me and because I had the opportunity to baby-sit for them for so long, it was hard not to feel that way. As the baby sitter, you are the acting adult and even though I was still a kid myself, I was responsible for them each night that I watched them. I took that responsibility very seriously and the parents trusted me to make sure the boys were safe while they went out.

It was a tough time for me after the younger boy died in that car accident. I would reflect on the night I was in that car accident in high school. I could have easily died that night and for some reason I did not. We all make mistakes and bad decisions whether you're in high school, college or as an adult. It is amazing to me that some people have to pay the ultimate price when making one mistake. Others, like myself, get second, third and many other chances to cheat death.

We all think that we are bulletproof and hearing about the loss of my friend hit close to home. This was the first person that I was really close to that would die. Over the next several years I would lose my eighty-year-old grandmother. This was devastating to me, but losing my young friend seemed worse because he was a twenty-one-year old boy in the prime of his life.

My heart goes out to his mom and dad who worked so hard trying to protect both their boys and keep them safe. The younger boy became an adult and this tragic accident happened. For some reason he did not get that second chance, and I ask all you young kids to remember that you are **not bulletproof**.

Life Lesson: *The decision that you make will lead to the action that you take so once again make it a positive outcome for goodness sake.*

As a parent today trying to raise two young boys, I want to share all my mistakes that I made while growing up, with them and all of you. It is not easy for me to be open and honest with you sharing my shortcomings. It is my hope that my two sons Jake and Josh learn from my mistakes and they avoid this destructive behavior altogether. I was lucky because I never hurt anyone or was hurt seriously while driving in a car back then and right up to the present.

Life Lesson: *Think for ten seconds before making a decision, it is your life.*

I am glad that the drunken driving laws have become stricter today because drunk drivers are not only killing themselves and their passengers, but also innocent people who they crash into while driving. It is a privilege to have a driver's license and we all must respect the laws of the road and become courteous drivers by avoiding accidents. It is a big responsibility when you drive a car and it is hard enough to drive while watching the road and today everyone has a cell phone. This is just another distraction for drivers.

Cell phone abuse, such as texting while driving, is becoming just as dangerous as drunk driving. These are major distractions and impair your ability to control your vehicle. Nothing good comes from drunk driving or texting on your cell phone while driving.

You are not only putting your life in danger but also any other innocent individual walking or driving on the road. We must respect the road and appreciate the awesome responsibility we have while operating a vehicle. I want Jake and Josh to remember these four driving life lessons.

Life Lesson: *The first is to take ten seconds and think before pulling out of a road when there is heavy traffic. You cannot rush while you are driving and only bad things will happen, so take your time, and if your late for something then it is better then not making it there at all.*

Life Lesson: *The second tip is to turn your cell phones off and keep them in your glove compartment. Only use them for emergencies or when you're out of the car and it is stopped. Pull into a safe location and off the road if you really need to make a call.*

Life Lesson: *The third tip is always buckling up while you are in a car. The seat belt is there to help keep you safe in the seat during an accident and may prevent you from being thrown out of the car. We never know when an accident may occur so it is important to be prepared.*

Life Lesson: *The fourth tip is to never take your eyes off the road especially when you want to change the radio station or roll down a window. It only takes a split second for your car to swerve into oncoming traffic and then both you and them are in trouble.*

I have been very lucky and fortunate not to have any accidents in twenty-eight years while driving on the road. That is a pretty good record and as I reflect back to high school and college once again, I remind myself about some mistakes that were made. I developed a bad behavior of drinking in excess on those Friday night parties with friends.

Apparently, my body became used to the weekend warrior behaviors that I had taught myself in high school and in college. As a married man raising two kids, I never got rid of that binge drinking behavior. It would seem that for the next twenty-three years after college my Friday night parties would continue into adulthood with family and friends. I would one day pay the price for abusing my body but once again I always thought that I was bullet proof and nothing bad would ever happen to me.

I turned forty-four years old at the stroke of midnight on Sunday September 21, 2009 lying on my back in a hospital bed. It was my last weekend of vacation before returning to work the next day and I apparently pushed my body to hard. The weekend started off with me playing thirty-six holes of golf on that previous Friday. I was having a great day with three other close friends. I would normally enjoy a few beers while playing golf, as it would help relax me and improve my golf game. When playing golf and having a few beers, the guys would call that swing oil. On that day I started off the first eighteen holes of golf by refusing to have any beer. My friends were shocked but understood as they enjoyed themselves to a few beers. I had to coach three baseball games the next day and decided that it would be best for me to stay away from drinking beer.

I played a horrible first eighteen holes, so as we started off for the next eighteen holes, I made a mistake and decided to have a couple of beers. Maybe that swing oil would help me improve for this next round. I ended up playing the second round of golf much better, but had a few more beers than I should have. I was on vacation and was caught up in the moment having fun with my three closest friends and the weekend warrior was back to his old habits.

I had forgotten all about my three baseball games that I had to coach the next day for Jake and Josh. I also did not drink any water and I was out in the sun all day playing golf.

Life Lesson: *Drinking beer does not hydrate your body while you're in the sun; it actually dehydrates you, which is not good.*

I got home later that Friday night, skipped dinner and went straight to bed. I knew I had a busy day on Saturday with the first baseball game starting promptly at eight A.M. I got up and had no time for breakfast and took my youngest son to the ball field. We had a double-header and the second game ended at noontime. I did not have any water during the double header.

I skipped lunch because I had to take my older son to his game, which was an hour away, and coach this game, which started at 1:30 P.M. We finished this game around 3:30 P.M. My son Jake and I stopped and had a late lunch together. This was the first meal that I had eaten in almost twenty-four hours and first glass of water.

I had spent all day in the sun playing golf on Friday and all day in the sun coaching three baseball games on Saturday and only had one bottle of water. Obviously, I did not drink any beer while coaching three baseball games on Saturday but also did not hydrate myself by drinking water. We got home Saturday night around six o'clock and I wanted to finish doing some chores around the house because I was returning to work on Monday. I decided to power wash my house and deck and completed those activities around nine o'clock that night.

Life Lesson: *Your body needs food and water to function properly like a car that needs gas to run.*

My wife had just finished making a nice Saturday night dinner and for some stupid reason, I declined to eat. My back was sore from standing all day coaching and working on the house, so I decided to jump into our hot tub. We have a nice hot tub on our deck, and I keep it at 104 degrees. To help me relax, I decided to have a few beers while soaking in the hot tub for about an hour. I felt great after an hour and went straight to bed skipping dinner all together. I awoke on that horrible and tragic Sunday morning feeling very weak. I had a good breakfast and decided to hang around the house that day relaxing. My wife took our older son to a basketball camp for a couple of hours.

My younger son and I watched the football game and during half time I decided to jump back in the hot tub for half an hour. I was not in the mood for any beer today because I was heading back to work the next day but once again I did not drink any water either. I finished watching the second half of the football game and I felt very weak.

I began to feel like I was going to pass out. I was feeling some tightness in my chest and having a difficult time breathing. I was short of breath and felt some numbness in my left arm, both legs, and pain in the back of my neck. I was sweating and knew that something was not right with my body.

I was home alone with my twelve-year old son and told him that I was not feeling well. I told him that if I passed out he would have to call 911. Josh was very upset because he said the color of my face was a grayish white color. I was embarrassed about the thought of an ambulance coming to my doorstep and thought that maybe these symptoms would just go away.

Like most men, we try to be brave and fight through any symptoms like the flu, but I knew something was not right. I called my Uncle Jack, a cardiologist and my primary care physician. I described the symptoms to him thinking that maybe I was having a heart attack. He advised me to call 911 immediately.

I did not feel up to driving to the hospital and did not want to call 911. I know that sounds crazy but I did not want an ambulance to come to the house. I asked my uncle to drive over and check me out because he was about a half hour away. I tried to relax and put cold water on my forehead. After about fifteen minutes, I collapsed. My son Josh picked up the phone and called 911 requesting an ambulance. My neighbor, who is a police officer, was the first person on the scene.

The ambulance arrived at my home and right behind them were my Uncle Jack and Auntie Marie. Jack did not like my symptoms that I had described to him on the telephone and knew that I was stubborn and would probably not call for an ambulance so he rushed over to my house. My Uncle Jack worked with the ambulance staff, helping prepare me for transport. Things were looking very bad for me and I was rushed into the hospital.

Life Lesson: *Never feel embarrassed to call 911 for help in any emergency*

I had every classic symptom of a massive heart attack from the pain in the back of the neck to the numbness in the left arm and legs. I had tightness in my chest and shortness of breath. My skin color was gray, my hands were cold and I was sweating.

They hooked up all the equipment to my body, checked my blood pressure and prepared my chest to use the paddles if necessary. I was transported to the hospital where my Uncle Jack worked and he followed.

In the emergency room I was shaking uncontrollably and I was completely numb from the waist down. I could not feel my legs and that is not a symptom of a heart attack. They confirmed that I did not experience a heart attack but had not idea why I was numb in my legs. I also had excruciating pain in my stomach and my blood pressure was extremely low. My uncle suggested that they take my blood and check for other factors that may cause the stomach pain and numbness in the legs. It was a good thing that my uncle ran my blood work because they discovered that **I had lost over 60 percent of the potassium in my body.**

All of my fluids were depleted and my potassium levels were so low that if not treated right away it was a possibility that I could die. I got so worked up thinking that I was having a massive heart attack I started hyperventilating and during that process, I had exhausted all of the CO_2 from my body. The loss of the CO_2 led to the pain in my stomach and numbness in my legs. Rapid CO_2 loss sometimes will occur with scuba divers coming up to fast from diving deep in the ocean and they call that the "*bends*."

My body was shutting down because of the extreme dehydration, potassium loss, and exhausted CO_2 in my body. The doctors began the process of bringing all my fluid levels back up to normal range over the next four to six hours. I would have to spend the night in the hospital so they could add potassium and water back into my body.

I turned forty-four years old in the hospital and that was a birthday I will never forget. It was a **perfect storm** of abusing my body for that whole weekend which started on that Friday. I deprived my body of water and food on Friday and Saturday while spending so much time out in the sun. Drinking beer and sitting in the hot tub at 104 degrees only helped to speed up the process of complete dehydration during that weekend. Drinking beer alone will dehydrate your body, sitting in a hot tub for that long alone will dehydrate you. I had done both, which is a bad combination and almost proved to be fatal.

Life Lesson: *Don't take life for granted your health is wealth.*

My uncle, Doctor Jack Klie, explained to me later that night in my hospital room that there was a good possibility that I could have died in my sleep Sunday night if I did not get to the hospital. He would go on to educate me about the importance of water and potassium in your body. These fluids are vital for all your organs to work properly, especially your heart.

Life Lesson: *Hot tubs are very dangerous and you should never spend more then twenty minutes in one and make sure that you drink plenty of water to hydrate your body.*

Our bodies cannot function properly without these fluids and I could have died in my sleep that night from a heart attack. The underlying reason for the heart attack would have been lack of fluids, which is 100 percent curable if recognized in time and corrected. I had deprived my body of the proper amount of food and water over this weekend. This is the first time that I had ever pushed my body to the brink of dehydration and exhaustion. I made some very bad decisions over this three-day weekend and almost accidentally killed myself in the process. I know that I am a weekend warrior but this was very irresponsible on my part.

Once again, I thought that I was invincible, bullet proof, and nothing bad will ever happen to me until it does. I know that a cat has nine lives but this time I had pushed the envelope too far. God had given me yet another chance and being forty-four years old now, it was time for me to make a life style change. I was not in high school or college anymore. I had a wife and two sons that needed me so I knew it was time for me to change.

I quit my weekend warrior rituals, drinking beer with family and friends. I began to walk every day and tried to get my body back into shape. As of today, I have not had a sip of beer since that scary Sunday and that has been seven months and still counting. I lost twenty-five pounds, and take it one day at a time. I look and feel so much better and want everyone to know that you can do the same thing. Learn from my very embarrassing mistake and never deprive your body of these vital fluids.

Life Lesson: *Never drink alcohol in a hot tub it can be a fatal combination.*

I have too much to live for and have no more time for beer. I never drank alcohol every day, but could not change my behavior or attitude toward drinking. I thought that I could continue to binge drink like I did in high school and college every Friday night with my friends and family. **Please learn from my mistake and don't push your body to those limits.**

Life Lesson: *Everything in moderation and respect your body with proper fluids.*

Health is wealth and all the money in the world is worthless for us if we don't take care of our body. We would all love to have financial freedom and one day become the richest person in the world. It does not mean anything if you are unhealthy and continue to abuse your body. What good is having a lot of money if you are not around to spend it?

Growing up as a kid, I was fearless and never thought anything bad would happen to me. I pushed my body to the limit and took it for granted. God blessed all of us with life. Our body is a temple and we need to learn that the body cannot function properly if it is deprived of the basic nutrients such as water and food.

Life Lesson: *Stop and smell the roses because life is precious. Don't wait for something bad to happen to you to make a change.*

As a child, my parents always reminded me that drinking water was important for good health. Our health teacher in school would say the same thing in class but do we all really understand and listen to this great advice? I think that it is safe to say that we all take our bodies for granted and we really do not understand the importance of water and other nutrients needed to keep us healthy.

I want my kids and all of you to understand that your body is made up of approximately 60 to 70 percent water. Your blood is mostly water, and your lungs, muscles, and brain all contain a lot of water in order for them to function properly. Your body needs water to help regulate body temperature so we don't overheat like your car engine.

We also need water to transport oxygen to our cells, joints, and organs and to help remove waste from the body. Water helps any nutrients that we take in such as potassium, as it will travel to all of these vital organs like your heart. Your body needs to have the right amount of potassium levels so it will function properly and if the levels are either too high or low it can be fatal.

I now eat a banana every day and make sure that I drink plenty of water and eat my three meals per day. I enjoy oatmeal for breakfast and put a banana and other fruit on top. I learned that every beer that you drink takes potassium out of your body and dehydrates you. If you have one beer then follow up with one bottle of water to hydrate yourself.

We can easily determine the amount of water our body needs by doing some simple math. Take your body weight in pounds and divide that number in half. That will give you the number of ounces of water per day that you will need to drink.

I weight 190 pounds and when you divide that in half it tells me that I need 95 ounces of water daily. The food that you eat will help make up around 20 percent of this and the rest you will need directly from drinking fluids such as water and juice. I need around twelve cups of water per day as a minimum.

If you drink alcohol, you should drink at least an equal amount of water. If you exercise you should drink another eight-ounce glass of water for every twenty minutes you are active. If you travel on an airplane, it is good to drink eight ounces of water for every hour you are on board the plane.

It is important for you to respect and care for your body and understand the symptoms of dehydration. This is the only body that God gave you. You lose water through urination, respiration, and by sweating. If you are very active then you will lose more water faster and need to replenish it. A strong odor to your urine, along with a yellow or amber color and leg cramps, indicate that you may not be getting enough water. Keep a bottle of water with you at all times.

Life Lesson: *We simply cannot survive without consuming enough water and nutrients daily. Your body is a temple so treat and respect it.*

Lenny Silva

I wanted to share with both my sons Jacob and Joshua and all of you yet another very embarrassing story about my life. This story goes out to all the young people and adults who may think that they can continue to deprive their bodies of the proper nutrients. I never knew how important potassium is to our body and helping to make our organs operate and function properly. How many second chances is God going to give to me?

As, I reflect back in my life and think about all that has happened during my younger days in high school, college and up to the present, I feel very blessed that I have been able to survive many difficult times and continue to get all these second chances. I know that it is for a reason and I believe that is for me to share them all with you. *My faults, mistakes and shortcomings will hopefully reach a child or adult and help guide them to make a life change.*

I want to educate my sons Jacob and Joshua all about the importance of taking care of their body. They need to learn from my mistakes and not repeat them as I fear that maybe them or any of you may not be as lucky. Knowledge is power and I don't want to scare them or any of you but these events really did occur in my life. They are not easy to talk about and share with the whole world but once again, I feel compelled to do just that with the sole intent that my story may save a life and the life it saves just might be yours.

I have opened up my heart and wear it on my sleeve exposing some very intimate details about my mistakes and shortcomings made during my life. These mistakes that I made, I take full responsibility for and they are something that **I am not proud of**. I cannot turn back the clock and change them but can be brave and share them all with you. If you take **ten seconds** and think before you act then you still have a chance not to follow in my footsteps.

That night while laying on my back in the hospital a local priest was making his rounds and he came into my room. He has been working and making patients happy for over thirty years at this particular hospital. He was a very funny person and every patient that he came into contact with had different ailments and he has seen them all over the years.

He had heard about my episode and bad decisions that I had made over the weekend and how I ended up where I was. We chatted for a few minutes and then he asked if it was ok to bless me and say a little pray on my behalf and I said yes and welcomed it.

The priest said God bless this **knucklehead** for he did not know what he was doing over the weekend and give him the strength to never make this same mistake again. Make sure that he tells as many people as possible and share his embarrassing story so maybe my second chance will save a life. It brought a tear to my eye and we shook hands as he left the room and went on his way preaching the good word of GOD.

I made a promise to God and myself that night to learn from my mistakes and help others.

Life Lesson: *Life is precious so enjoy every minute and respect your body never taking it for granted.*

Eighth Inning

Understanding the Importance of Money and Investing

I was fortunate enough to grow up in a loving home with two parents, two sisters and a brother, living in a nice quiet neighborhood. In those days we never had to worry about locking your doors. It was always a goal for my parents to provide their children with more opportunities in life than they received from their parents.

I like that philosophy and that is what I am trying to do for my sons Jacob and Joshua. I want to help prepare them for life by giving them all the tools and education they will need to become successful. I think we all want that for our kids.

I was the first child on both my parents' side of the family to go and graduate from college. I was able to accomplish that goal because of the sacrifices my parents made for me. I want to take that one step further with my kids and help them not only graduate from college, but also become financially secure in their lives and I have the same hope for all of you.

I have been working in the financial services field for over twenty-three years. I am a licensed financial advisor and have helped many people manage and grow their investments. I enjoyed finance classes in college and after graduating, continued and advanced my knowledge and career in that field.

My parents would both work hard trying to manage all the household expenses and buying nice things for their four kids. It seemed like we never went without anything, but back then the price for goods and services were much cheaper then they are today.

I still remember hearing my parents talk about money and we did go through tough times like most families experience. They were just making enough for us to get by and they were able to raise all of us in this nice town, which had a great school system.

I began at a very early age reading and trying to learn as much as I could about money. I heard all about it growing up from my parents. I figured that if I wanted to have nice things in the future then I better get a good understanding of this thing we all call money.

I will not be able to teach all of you everything that there is to learn about money and investing in this one chapter. There is just too much to cover but I want to at least share with Jacob and Joshua and the rest of the world some basic finance.

I recommend that all of you study and read as much that you can about planning for your future and investing. It is your money, you work hard to earn it, now work hard to protect it. It is your responsibility to make sure that you understand how to invest and manage your money wisely. You can get a free consultation from an investment advisor at your local bank, so take an hour to listen and learn all you can from them.

Life Lesson: *Money does make the world go round.*

We need money to buy all those products and services that we all use everyday. I still remember my parents say how expensive things were and when we were kids the prices were so much cheaper then there are today. We all heard a grandparent say, "When I was a kid that product was so much cheaper, a loaf of bread only cost six cents."

The price for a gallon of milk when I was growing up in 1970 was around .99 cents compared to that same gallon of milk today, which is $2.99. That same gallon of milk only cost .50 cents back in 1934. In 1934 a pair of men's slacks was $1.94 compared today for $39.95.

The point is over time the price of goods and services will increase because of inflation, which usually runs around three percent per year. So we all need to understand that our money will lose purchasing power in the future. Inflation decreases the amount of goods and services you would be able to purchase in the future if you are not earning enough on your investment.

I want Jake and Josh to understand the value of money and how inflation can affect the purchasing power that it may have on goods and services. The price for products and services may have been cheaper during my grandfather's years, but the income they earned was also much lower.

We all need to understand that investing our money with the right types of investments is important so that it grows enough to outpace inflation. **Purchase power risk** is the risk that money will lose its purchasing power over time. The purchasing power risk is also referred to as the **inflationary risk**.

Do you think that the price of goods and services will increase or decrease in the future? The cost of goods and services will increase over time, therefore we must consider those investments that will help our money grow and try to outpace inflation over time.

We have many types of investments to choose from. Conservative investments such as a bank savings account and a CD, are a couple that are most susceptible to purchasing power risk otherwise know as inflationary risk. They do not offer you big enough returns on your money and they do not outpace inflation which runs around three percent.

You run the risk of not earning enough interest on your investments and as the price of goods and services increase over time due to inflation, we all run the risk of not keeping up. The key is to establish a diversified portfolio that meets your overall risk tolerance level as an investor and earn around six to eight percent return on your money.

A financial advisor can help meet your short and long term goals with recommendations on different investment choices that will outpace inflation. They will also make sure the investment is suitable for you and meets your risk tolerance level.

Life Lesson: *A penny saved is a penny earned. Invest wisely so you can earn dollars and not pennies.*

The investments that offer the best opportunities over the long term have traditionally been growth stocks or growth mutual funds. These are the types of investments that over long term, like ten-year periods, can return six or eight percent on money that you invest. These are the types of investments that have outpaced inflation and we need to consider them in our diversified portfolio.

In 1934, the price of a new car was $445. Compared to today, the price would be $13,500. In 1934, the price for a pound of prime rib roast was twenty-seven cents and today it is $6.99 for that same pound. A loaf of bread was six cents in 1934, compared to that same loaf of bread today for 1.59.

We all need to understand that that you work hard to make money. You need to learn some basic knowledge about money so that you can have control over your life, which revolves all around money. We all need money to buy food, shelter, clothing, and gas for our car so that we can drive to work. These are just some of our basic necessities we need to live on and when you have a family these cost will only increase.

We would all like to enjoy some luxuries during our lifetime. We would like to one day purchase our own home, a nice car, take a vacation to an exotic island, and retire at a time that you can actually still be walking, so you can enjoy it. All of your dreams, wants, and goals revolve around money and investing.

I believe that all of you have the ability to learn and manage your own money. You need to understand that it is your money and it will have a direct affect on the quality of your life. I am not saying here that having a lot of money will buy you happiness. It is just something that we all should have some basic knowledge about so we can make better choices and reach those goals that you may have set in your life.

In school all your classes are important, but take the time to listen and study Economics. That is the subject that will help give all of you a good foundation when learning about money. **Micro Economics** and **Macro Economics** are the courses where you can begin to understand all about the flow of money in our economy and the mechanics of that process.

Interest rates, economic growth, unemployment and inflation are those terms that we hear about in the news every day. I would guess that most of you really do not understand these concepts and how they impact our lives daily. You also hear about the stock market all the time. These concepts have a direct affect on stocks, both increasing and decreasing in value. The Dow was up or down today by how many points is something that you will hear about every night while watching the news on TV.

Life Lesson: *You can learn about money by reading the business section of the newspaper and not the sports section. The Dow stands for Dow Jones Industrial Average (DJIA) and it tracks 30 large cap blue chip stocks.*

Interest rates are a leading indicator and direct affect on the cost of borrowing money. When interest rates are higher, then people tend to hold off buying larger items such as homes and cars because in the end, it costs them more money. They have to pay more in interest when these rates are higher.

The stock market will tend to go lower when the interest rates are higher because people tend to sell their stocks, anticipating that the overall market is heading down and the economy may be growing too fast.

When the interest rate is lower then people tend to buy these larger items because it does end up costing them less in the long run. When people in the country buy more houses, cars, and clothing then our economy grows. When the economy grows then jobs are created and unemployment goes down.

The stock market will tend to go higher when interest rates are lower because people tend to buy more stocks anticipating that the market may be heading higher as the economy is beginning to slow. People look to the stock market to get better returns on their money considering banks are not paying that much for savings accounts when rates are lower.

The stock market can move up and down based on many leading indicators other than just interest rate moves. If our country has to deal with a terrorist attack like we had on September 11, 2001, that event and bad news will send the market plummeting. People become afraid and once fear sets into the stock market it will go down.

The events that occurred on September 11, 2001 are considered to be out of the control of any investor. It was a global event that affected every stock market that operates in the world, sending them all down. History has shown that every time the stock market went down drastically from tragic events, it would always return higher over time.

When we have low unemployment, skilled labor becomes important. Because of high demand, employers will pay higher wages to retain their services. Incomes will rise for this skilled labor. The higher wages that we all earn are great, but we also need to understand that lower unemployment and rising wages contribute to inflation.

I just finished telling you about inflation and how that will increase the prices for products and services in the future. Inflation occurs at times of lower unemployment because as more people work and make more money, prices go up, partially because company's costs have increased for paying those higher wages.

If inflation occurs in the economy then interest rates will rise. The government will raise interest rates when the economy is showing signs of higher inflation in order to slow down people from buying and curb the growth of the economy. It all sounds a little confusing

Life Lesson: *Read as much as you can about economics and investing.*

What seems good for you as a worker, lots of jobs and higher wages, may be bad for an investor because it could lead to higher interest rates and lower returns on the stock market. People tend to sell off the stock market when interest rates go higher and they may seek other conservative investments at your local bank like certificate of deposits, otherwise known as a CD.

The Federal Reserve Bank is always trying to strike a balance between setting the proper interest rates and growing the economy, but at a moderate pace. They don't want the economy to grow too fast because inflation may set in and when the economy is really slow like we are experiencing today, they try to lower interest rates to get it jump-started.

The Federal Reserve Bank, simply known as "The Fed", has a chairman whose name is Ben Bernanke. The "Fed" is our country's central bank located in Washington, D.C. They oversee all the banks in the United States, and they have the power to change the rate of interest at which smaller banks borrow from the "Fed"

Most banks in our country borrow money from "The Fed" at what they call a discount rate and the "Fed" charges those banks interest. The "Fed" will meet on average four times per year and based on the economy and leading indicators, will decide if they want to raise or lower this rate.

We also have what is called the federal funds rate and the prime rate. The federal funds rate is the interest that one bank is charged by another bank when they want to lend money to each other. The "Fed" does not set this rate in stone but can influence it by adding reserves to or taking them away from banks.

If the "Fed" decides to put more money into circulation, then it will cost a bank less to borrow from another bank and if they decide to take money out of circulation, it will cost the bank more money to borrow. It revolves around supply and demand. When we have more supply of something like money, it is cheaper for banks to borrow. When we have less supply of something like money and higher demand for it, then it costs more.

I still remember one Christmas my oldest sister Janene loved those cabbage patch dolls. There was such a high demand for this product and low supply of them in the shopping malls they were almost impossible to buy. The stores selling them knew this and doubled the price of them. People did not care about paying the higher price because they were hard to get. Supply and demand for all products, including money, works the same way.

The prime rate is the interest rate banks charge their most significant customers. The "Fed" sets this rate and that announcement is a major leading indicator for the stock market. Your local bank can set their rates off this prime rate and customers typically pay a few percentage points higher. You can find the present prime rate in the Wall Street Journal or business section of any major newspaper.

Life Lesson: *We should all at least know what the current prime rate is.*

It is safe to say that the chairman of the Federal Reserve is a very powerful person and some believe even more powerful than the President of the United States. The main reason is that our economy can slow down or speed up at any time. The Federal Reserve studies these leading indicators on a regular basis and after they meet, they announce any interest rate moves.

The stock market is always very interested to learn what the Federal Reserve will do with interest rates after they have a meeting, because their decisions can have either a negative or positive affect on the stock market. The "Fed" is also making sure that we have an open and free marketplace where there is enough liquidity in the marketplace, helping to keep money flowing.

For those people who are invested in the stock market, two categories of the market are described as either a bear or bull market. A bear market means that the market is experiencing a downturn and a bull market means that it is going up. Both distinctions are determined by a move of twenty-percent in either direction.

If the market is moving up by twenty percent over a period of time, then you will hear people in the news refer to it as a bull market or the bulls are running. This means that the stock market is running higher. When the opposite occurs and we have a decline in the market by twenty percent over a period of time, then we are in a bear market.

A stock is a company that has issued shares to the public and people buy and sell those shares of the company when the stock market is open for business. Anyone who has visited Disney World should know that company trades on the stock market. The more people who travel to Disney World the more profits that company will earn. The better the earnings for that company the higher the stock price can go.

If you bought 100 shares of Disney at $30 per share it would cost you $3,000 as an investment. You hold the stock for ten years and over that time frame the stock price would have gone up to $60 per share because the company has performed well, and their earnings have increased because many people continued to visit the park.

If you sold your 100 shares at $60 per share it is worth $6,000 and you made $3,000 on your initial investment. If the stock pays a dividend, which is like interest, such as four percent, and you re-invest that dividend to buy more shares over that ten-year period, then you would have more than the original 100 shares and your profit would be more.

People will always say that they are afraid to invest in the stock market and it is only a gamble. There is so much to learn about the stock market. People need to understand that the products we use everyday are included in the stock market. When we purchase them, we are contributing to the earnings of these companies and it affects the stock price.

Life Lesson: *You worked hard for your money now make sure it works hard for you.*

Every day we wake up and use products that companies make and are traded on the stock market. We take a shower and use **Dove** soap, brush our teeth and use **Colgate** toothpaste, eat our **Frosted Flakes** breakfast cereal, put on our clothes from **American Eagle** and ride in a car to go to school made by **Volvo**.

Just think the next time you walk through a mall, almost every company in there is trading on the stock market. People can invest their money through a broker and buy shares in these companies. A very famous investor used to go to the mall with his kids. He would follow his kids into their favorite store and once inside, the investor noticed the store was packed with people.

That investor would then go back to his office and begin to research that company and looked at how much they earned. He saw first hand all the people buying products from that store including his kids, so he would buy the stock. He made a lot of money doing this because he knew that the more products a company sold, the more money they made and the stock would rise over time.

One of the advantages of investing in stocks over time is growth, providing that you have selected the right stocks. Compared with other investments vehicles such as bonds, gold, real estate, and treasuries, stocks have provided investors with the best annual investment returns. During a forty-year period from 1960 through 1996, the average annual return was eleven percent.

The disadvantage can be considerable, depending on the performance of the company whose stock you have purchased. There is no guarantee that you will make money by investing in stocks. If you buy a stock and that company goes bankrupt then you can lose all the money that you put into that one stock. You must do some research and make sure that the company is solid before you invest.

A very popular way for the average investor to participate in the stock market is to buy a **mutual fund**. Most people are uncomfortable buying an individual stock so they would look into buying shares in a growth mutual fund. A mutual fund is investors who pool all their money and buy shares in a particular mutual fund. The mutual fund may have fifty companies that make up the portfolio.

Your risk is diversified because you now have invested your money buying shares of a mutual fund, which own stocks in fifty companies instead of you trying to invest money yourself in just one company. The mutual funds usually have a mutual fund manager who does the research and he will buy and sell companies trying to grow the share price of the mutual funds for all the investors.

A good example of a mutual fund is a package of all these companies that we see in a shopping mall. The mutual fund will hold fifty different companies that you walk into while visiting a mall. Each company will have a different performance, some better than others, but as a group we are looking for overall performance to average up.

If you invest all of your money in one stock and that company is not performing that well, have low earnings and go out of business, then you can end up losing all your money. That is why when investing in a mutual fund you are putting your money into a fund that pools all other investors' money, and the mutual fund manager does all the work selecting many stocks.

Jacob and Joshua, along with many others kids and parents, enjoy using Face Book. This was a great idea by a young twenty-one year old genius. This young man had an idea and formed a company. He then took his company public and sold shares of it on the stock market. This company has done extremely well for any investors who bought shares in the stock especially when it first came out.

The young twenty-one year old is now a multi-billionaire. He had the idea and started the company and took it public, making himself a lot of money. We have seen many young people do similar things with companies such as Microsoft, Yahoo, Google, Amazon.com, Ebay, and Oracle. Those company founders are all multi-billionaires.

The most successful investor of our time is Warren Buffet. He has created a company called Berkshire Hathaway. Warren is the second richest man in the world. This company has been around for about fifty years. I read an article in the paper about a couple that had invested $50,000 into this one stock when it first came out.

They did not touch the investment and let it sit for fifty years and as the share price of the company kept growing over time, so would their return on the investment. The share price on this stock rose to $100,000 per share. The couple finally sold all their shares when they retired and it was worth around $600 million dollars.

I make no guarantee that you will make that kind of returns on your investment. I will say that it is absolutely impossible to make anything close to that by investing all of your money in a bank account or CD, which only pay 1 percent interest.

Time is the most important factor in the growth of your money. The more time your money has to grow and the more time you spend making careful decisions about it today, the more money you will likely have when you retire. Planning and investing for your future is important and the sooner you start the better off you will be.

I know that investing in the stock marker sounds very complicated, and that is why the experts will always remind people that it is for the long term. Over the long term, investing in stocks and stock mutual funds do offer the best annual returns on your money.

Life Lesson: *Don't put all your eggs in one basket; diversify.*

There are many different types of mutual funds such as Growth, Income, Growth and Income, Balanced and International. Each of these funds have objectives and the mutual fund manager is responsible for making sure that they buy companies that will meet those objectives and produce solid returns to the shareholders.

There may be different types of companies that will be included in a growth fund and not in an international fund. If you are investing in an international fund, you are seeking to invest in companies located outside the United States.

There are also different sized companies that can be included in funds. They are small capitalization otherwise known as "small cap", mid size capitalization otherwise known as "mid cap" and Large companies as "large cap". These classifications help to narrow which type of funds a person will want to make up their diversified portfolio.

The large cap funds are those largest companies such as IBM, General Electric, Microsoft, Wal-Mart, Target, which have billions in financial size. The small to mid cap companies are those smaller companies that have the potential to grow into large cap companies over time.

The smaller cap growth funds are more risky for an investor because they are not as mature as a large cap, but also offer better opportunities to grow your money more quickly over time as they increase in size. Diversification is investing your money over all the different classes of funds. You are spreading your money and lowering your overall risk by investing in different fund classes.

If you are a twenty-year old with a ten-year time horizon and have an aggressive risk tolerance level and have $10,000 dollars to invest, you may want to spread your money out this way. You may invest some of your money in small cap, mid cap, large cap, and international growth funds. If you had $10,000 to invest you may put 30% or $3,000 in the small cap, then 20% or $2,000 in the mid cap, 20% or $2,000 in the large cap, 30% or $3,000 international. This is only an illustration and you should consult with a professional before investing to make sure it meets your risk tolerance level and it is suitable for you.

You can always create a mock investment portfolio. This is what I call lets pretend portfolio but a fun way to learn about the market and tracking your investments. If you take the business section of the paper you will see all the companies listed along with their stock symbols. You can pretend to be your own mutual fund manager and you have $100,000 of money you would like to invest. Let us create your own mutual fund and you decide which companies' stocks you want to purchase. Which companies do you want to purchase? A great rule of thumb is to stick with companies that you know. If you can explain about any particular company to a ten-year, then you have a good idea of what that company does.

Life Lesson: *Invest in companies that you know and understand how they work prior to investing any of your money.*

Once you decide on the companies that you would like to buy stock in for your own **mock** mutual fund portfolio, then do some research and take a look at their earnings. You want to know if they are showing a profit year after year. Once we get some of that information then you can make a better decision if you want to invest your money.

Let us take a look at some companies that you all have heard of and probably purchased a product or service from. The companies that we all know about are **Wal-Mart, Disney, American Eagle, Target, Microsoft** has the Xbox, **Nintendo** has the Wii. **Verizon** has cell phones, **Google** is an Internet provider, when we shop on line we use **E-bay** and **Amazon.com.**

Face Book to see our friends, **Comcast** or **COX** cable TV provider, **Twitter** for leaving your messages on line, **Apple** has the IPOD, Itunes and the computer; **Sony** has the Play Station three video game systems along with great TV's. **Abercrombie and Fitch** for clothing, **McDonald's, Sub-Way, Wendy's, Burger King,** and **Dunkin Donuts** to eat.

Coca Cola, have a coke and a smile, **Pepsi, Poland Springs, Ocean Spray, Dell** computers, **Intel** makes the chip to help the computer run, **Colgate** toothpaste. By using these thirty companies that are highlighted, you could spread your $100,000 and buy some shares in each of their stock for your mock mutual fund portfolio. You have just done what a mutual fund manager does everyday.

If you still don't think that you need to know anything about the stock market or investing your money, then just stop and think about all the products and services that you spend your money on every day. Open your mind and embrace that the stock market is a part of all our lives and understand the importance it can play in your future.

Understand the importance of money and investing. It is your money to make and yours to invest and grow. I want you to reach those goals that you have set forth like buying a home, car, college expenses or retiring comfortably. I want to make everyone aware that you can spend a little time every day reading and learning about money and the importance it has on our daily lives.

Here are some very good mutual fund families and they offer all the different types of funds to meet your needs and risk tolerance level. They are **Fidelity** (800) 353-4881, **Vanguard** (800) 997-2798, **Janus** (800) 525-3717, and **T. Rowe Price** (866) 586-0088. You can call any one of these for a free brochure and informational booklet and the phone representatives are available to help with any of your questions.

You can also visit your local bank and ask to set up an appointment with their financial advisor and receive a free consultation. The financial advisor will ask you a series of questions to learn about all your dreams, wants and goals for the future. They will help to determine your risk tolerance level and then make a suitable recommendation for investing your money.

Life Lesson: *Get a financial check up today just like we all do regularly with a doctor.*

Ninth Inning

Control Your Debt and Spending Habits

I remember a major league baseball player who had a twenty-year career and earned millions of dollars along the way. He was recently in the news because he had to file for bankruptcy. He had bought thirty luxury cars and extravagant homes all over the world.

This athlete had to file bankruptcy because he owed more in debt then he had in assets and could no longer afford to pay the monthly payments on everything that he bought. He also accumulated two hundred thousand dollars in credit card debt.

He had lost all control over his spending habits and debt purchases, thinking that the money he was making would just keep rolling in. His baseball career was over and he had no other job that could generate enough income to support this life style that he had created. He did not plan for the future and invest the millions of dollars that he had earned during his career. He just kept spending money on purchases that he really did not need. He racked up such an incredible amount of debt and was left with no choice but to file for bankruptcy protection. This happens to plenty of professional sport athletes.

He had to sell off all those homes and cars trying to repay all the banks that lent him money. In the end, he was left with nothing and he lost it all. He blew millions of dollars on luxury items and lived the high life for twenty years. He is now broke. He is too old to play baseball and no major league team will offer him a contract. He did not graduate from college and has no experience in the workplace. He was once famous and considered to be an idol to millions of kids and now can't afford to pay rent for an apartment. He had to move back home with his parents at the age of forty-two.

It is a sad story and he is not alone. Millions of people in our country get into financial difficulty because they over-extend themselves and acquire too much debt. The biggest debt for Americans today is **credit card debt**. Those credit card companies will keep sending pre-approval notices to Americans and we keep saying yes. The average American has $8,000 dollars in credit card debt.

Millions of Americans carry several credit cards in their wallets and some people may have ten credit cards and owe balances on each of them. This excessive credit card debt is a burden and will take these people their entire life to pay off in full if they only make the minuim-required payment each month.

If you owe $4,000 on a credit card and they are charging you 18% interest and you made the minimum monthly payment, say $50 dollars per month, it would take you around **40 years** to pay that credit bill off in full. It would also cost you thousands of dollars in finance charges based on the interest you have to pay.

Life lesson: *Live within your means don't spend what you don't have.*

I want Jacob, Joshua, and you to understand the emotions that surround debt. We all have **needs** and **wants** in our lives. Our emotions drive our wants and everybody wants to have nice things such as homes, cars, diamonds, clothes, and vacations. We do not need to have thirty luxury cars and the mistake that athlete made is he let all of his wants influence his decision over his true needs. How you spend your money is always a personal decision and we all may view items as "necessities" in a different manner. We technically only need food, water, clothing, and shelter to survive. We all have heard the phrase "***tough love***" and this chapter is exactly that. I am giving my two sons information so it will help them and all of you with a better understanding about debt and spending habits. I am not trying to tell anyone how he or she should live their lives but only trying to point out that if we make the debt then be prepared to pay for it.

If you can't pay off your credit card bill in full each month then you are charging to many items to it. You are spending much more money then you are taking in every month. You are falling into the emotional trap of **wanting** items that you really don't need and using that credit card and accumulating debt that you can't afford. If you can't payoff that $4,000 dollars in credit card debt that you owe right now in full, then you are in **financial trouble**. The athlete who ended up owing two hundred thousand dollars in credit card debt started off owing just a small amount like $4,000.

We forget that just because we don't have to pay for these products at the point of sale when we hand the merchant our credit card, we think it is free. We think because we are not handing them cash over the counter, it is not a problem. We think we will pay it later when the bill comes in. The bill will keep coming in month after month until the whole balance is paid in full. You keep adding a new purchase every month and your balance grows higher.

The credit card company wants you to only pay the minimum of $50 per month because they are making 18% interest month after month on all your unpaid balances. Once you carry a monthly balance and then continue to make charges on that card every month then two things happen. Your bill grows higher because you have not paid the outstanding balance in full the previous month and then your monthly finance charges increase based on the interest rate they are charging you. Credit card companies make money on finance charges.

I have had credit cards for twenty-five years now and always **make the payment in full each month**. I set up a monthly budget plan which will outline for me exactly how much money each month my debt exposure will be and subtracting that from my monthly take home net pay. I have been fortunate and disciplined to make sure that my credit card bills are paid in full every month. The major advantage for all of us as consumers when you pay the credit card bill off in full each month is the monthly finance charges you **will not** incur. The monthly interest rates your credit card company charges you will not matter, if you're paying that bill off in full every month.

Life Lesson: *There is a solution to every problem including your finances.*

If you have credit card debt with a large balance and cannot pay the bill off in full then don't panic. Take a moment and begin to track your spending habits and how you spend money everyday. Keep a money diary or journal writing down each day the items that you purchase and the cost associated with them. Try to change your behaviors and begin to cut out buying a large cup of coffee every day and set up a plan to aggressively start making extra payments on that credit card debt. If you are paying 18% percent interest on credit card debt and somehow work to pay that bill off in full over time then you just made 18% percent on your money because this is the interest rate you would have paid out of pocket by keeping the balance.

Start to ask yourself a question; what is my true **need** for a credit card? My answer is **convenience**. I only use the credit card as a convenience, because it is **safer** then carrying around cash. I use my credit card to pay for gas at the pump, which allows me to get in and out much more quickly then visiting the cashier inside, and paying cash. Another need or benefit of having a credit card is when you're traveling. You are unable to rent a car without one and it is more convenient when you purchase a plane ticket and book a hotel room. The whole world is getting away from cash and becoming electronic so it is important for all of us to get control of our spending habits and monthly debt.

Life Lesson: *Set a monthly budget and only spend what your net take home pay is. Spend your money wisely on those things you need, want, and enjoy.*

The major problem with credit card debt is the simple fact it is **not your only bill** you have to pay every month. You have to pay **rent** or **a mortgage payment** for your home. You have to **pay insurance** for everything including **health care**, **home, auto** and **life insurance** to protect your loved ones, if you die unexpectedly. You have to **make a car payment** for that nice new car that you drive to work everyday.

You have to **pay for your utilities** in the home that you live in, including **gas or oil**, **electric**, and **cable for your TV**. We all have a **cell phone** and each month those bills are getting higher and higher, especially if you text a lot and exceed limits they allow. You need to eat every day and have to **pay for food**.

You need to **pay for gas** in that new car, so you can get to work and don't forget about all the **taxes** that you have to pay. You have to pay taxes for everything just like insurance. You have **auto excise taxes** due to the town where you park the car. You have to **pay property taxes** on your home to the town where you live if you own the house.

You have **payroll taxes** including **social security**, **state** and **federal** that comes out of your paycheck every month. These taxes reduce the amount of take-home pay, otherwise known as net pay. You have to pay a **water bill** to the town that supplies water to your home if you own it.

You have to pay for **clothing, shoes, socks, underwear, soap, shampoo, and toothpaste.** You have to pay for the **furniture** that you sit on, the **TV** that you watch. You have to pay for your **college tuition,** or maybe you are lucky and received a scholarship. You have to pay for **books** at college for each class that you take.

You have to **pay for everything** and these items are not free. We don't need to burden ourselves with more debt with credit cards. There is plenty of debt waiting for you each month. I don't want to make any of you afraid by listing all of these bills, but understand that these are the monthly debt payments your parents have to deal with.

It is fine to **want** luxury items, but you need to live within your means. If you simply don't make enough money to pay for these items that you **want,** then you have to be disciplined enough to say no. It is becoming too easy for people to reach in their pocket and use that credit card, knowing they don't have to pay cash at the point of sale.

Life Lesson: *Find a balance in your life and everything in moderation including how we spend our money. The next time you're at the mall and you feel the urge to splurge and buy that third pair of shoes. Stop and take ten seconds and think do I really need them.*

Most people think that they can afford to pay for those luxury items when the credit card bill comes in at the end of the month, and forget about all their other bills. They don't pay the credit card bill in full and they keep buying more items, and the balance explodes higher and higher. I suggest that we set a monthly budget and get a really good understanding of what the total current monthly bills are. We can write down on a piece of paper the dollar amount owed for each bill and which date they are due for payment each month. The following is just an example of a typical family monthly budget.

Your electric bill is $200 dollars and due on the 5th of every month. Gas bill is $300 and due on the 10th of every month. Cable bill, which is a bundle package and covers TV, Internet, and Phone, is $200 per month and due on the 15th of every month. Mortgage or rent is $2,000 per month and due on the 20th of every month. Car payment is $300 and due on the 25th of every month.

You also need to consider the other essentials like food, gas, and coffee on the way to work, so figure another $400 per month for these items. Your total monthly debt just to cover your basic needs to live is $3,400. That is a lot of money and you have not even used that credit card yet to go shopping.

Then you should write down exactly what the monthly take home net pay is. For example, we will assume it is $4,400. Budgeting your money means that you will make sure that you have enough take home net pay to handle your current monthly debt. If you are taking home $4,400 each month, then that means that you are making around $80,000 dollars annually.

Life Lesson: *Don't spend more then you make. Keep credit card purchases in control.*

If you have excess cash left over after paying all your current monthly debt obligations, then we call that extra cash disposable income. Disposable income is extra income used to buy all those items that you **want.** You can use that extra money to treat yourself and buy something that will make you happy.

In our example you have $1,000 left over each month. It may sound like a lot of money but don't forget that you have to pay for insurance and excise tax on the car, home insurance and property taxes on your home if you own it. These are usually annual expenses and people tend to forget about them. We think that we had $1,000 in excess each month and felt good, so we go out and use that credit card. We start buying items we want and figure that we will pay that bill off in full every month. That is the game plan and then those other annual bills come due that month and you have to decide which bill is more important.

Life Lesson: *You will find a sample monthly budget form under the extra innings section of this book. You can customize this form to make it work best for you and your lifestyle.*

I need to pay the car and home insurance bill. I need to pay the property and car taxes, so we end up making the minimum $50 dollar credit card payment. **That is where people get into trouble because they think that they have extra disposable income and they don't.**

Life Lesson: *Make sure you account for all bills so you can set the correct budget.*

Credit card companies will begin to target our children when they turn eighteen years old and enter college. Credit card companies will offer these kids pre-approved credit cards up to $4,000 knowing full well that they may be in college and don't have a job.

Credit card companies want to get you started on the path of debt and they want to be **first in line**. They know that you will have all those other bills that I mentioned waiting for you later. They want to get you hooked first and begin owing them money. They want you to enjoy yourself and start using that credit card. Credit card companies set the highest interest rates allowable by law to the students. You don't have to indicate on the credit card application that you are working and have no income to qualify for the card. Remember that on this application, you will need to supply the company with your social security number, date of birth and home address. They justify offering college students these cards by charging these ridiculously high rates.

The rates can be 18, 20 or even 25 percent monthly interest, if you maintain a balance and don't pay that bill in full every month. You are going to college to earn a higher education and better prepare yourself for a career in the workplace. You need to be prepared for all these special offers and understand that you are being targeted. It is sad to read in the newspaper about some young adults who racked up high credit card bills while in college and with all the pressure of school work and this added stress they placed on themselves some students did commit suicide.

Life Lesson: *Suicide is never an option and trust your parents. Together you will find a viable solution to any financial, emotional, or other problem* *that maybe bothering you. Life is precious and never let anyone or anything push you to those extreme limits. Please give your parents that chance to help you before you take what GOD has given you and that is life. The game of life is sometimes cruel but a solution awaits every problem.*

I now have scared you enough about credit cards and went over all the **disadvantages** that they have. I just want you to be prepared for all these offers that you will be getting in the mail once you turn eighteen and go off to college. You need to remember that if you don't have a job or income, then how can you pay any bill such as a credit card.

I want my sons Jacob and Joshua and all of you **not to be afraid of debt or money**. I just want you all to understand and respect debt and your responsibility for creating it and paying for it. It is important for you to start your financial education. I want you to know and understand how these cards work and if you have a balance owed they will continue to charge you each month until you pay them in full. Treat all debt with respect just like you would any person because money and debt are important and powerful.

Despite all the potential disadvantages that I shared with all of you, I believe that like everything in life there are **some advantages** to getting a credit card. The advantages of getting **one credit card** are to help you begin to build a credit profile. The card is there for you in the event of an emergency, such as a plane ticket home for the holidays or to rent a car because you don't like to fly.

It is important to begin to establish credit for yourself and when you pay that monthly balance off in **full every month** it gets reported to the credit reporting agencies. The credit reporting agencies maintain the payment history on everyone who has been issued credit. They are also known as the credit bureau.

As a college student or young adult eighteen years of age or older, applying for one pre-approved credit card **can be a good idea**, since the older you get, the harder it maybe to qualify. If you are out of college, then those companies will need to verify your income.

Life Lesson: *Take advantage of one pre-approved credit card with a small credit limit.*

There are credit bureaus and credit reports that keep track of the payment history of all people who use credit cards, department store issued cards, bank car loans, student loans and bank mortgage loans. When you pay these bills on time every month, you are in the credit scoring system maintained at the credit bureau.

This rating system is essentially universal and all lenders, employers, and landlords will pull your credit report to determine your credit worthiness. They can make a more informed decision if they want to lend you any money or rent you their home to live in. The credit bureaus track everyone by your name, social security number, birth date and home address.

You are entitled to receive one free credit report every 12 months upon request. You are also entitled to a free credit report if you are unemployed and plan to look for a job within sixty days, if you are on welfare or if your report has mistakes because of fraud or identity theft. Otherwise, a consumer reporting agency my charge you a nominal fee for another copy of your report within the twelve-month period. I believe that you all should look at your credit report at least once a year just to make sure that it is accurate. This is also the main reason why you need to protect your personal information such as social security number and birth date so your identity will not be stolen. People will take your information and pretend that they are you and apply for credit everywhere and skip out on the bill.

The credit reporting agencies have what they call a FICO score. FICO is the short name for Fair Isaac Company, which created it. This is a number generated and assigned to each individual. **The better your credit, the higher your FICO score.**

The higher the FICO score the less risk you are to a lender. The lower the FICO score the more risk you are to a lender. The FICO scores range from a low of 350 to a high of 900. The best way to raise your score is to pay your monthly bills when they come in and get those payments to the lenders prior to the due date.

Your FICO credit score is a direct correlation to who you are. A higher FICO score indicates that person is responsible and conscientious about paying their bills on time. Your FICO score can be considered a benchmark to determine your character, integrity and reputation. Perception is everything especially when you're trying to get a job. Many employers who will run a background check prior to offering you a job can learn much by somebody's FICO score. If the FICO score is to low they may decide that you are a risk and not offer you the job. Your FICO credit score follows you everywhere so it is important to make sure that it is accurate and your working hard to maintain a good score.

Life Lesson: *Understand the importance of your FICO score; monitor your credit file on a regular basis to make sure it is accurate, which will help protect your identity.*

You will not have a credit bureau file and no FICO score, if you have not been issued credit. This is the main advantage and why I recommend that you take advantage of one pre- approved credit card when you turn eighteen. It will help you begin to establish a credit bureau file and make sure that you pay the bill on time each month. Make sure that the lender has your correct billing address. You may be putting your home address on the application but need to receive the bill at the college, which is located someplace else. If you don't get the bill, then you won't be able to pay it on time and the credit card company reports all late payments to the credit bureau.

Life Lesson: *Late payments reported to the credit bureau drive down your FICO score.*

Once you turn sixteen years old and with a parent as a co-signer, you will be able to open a checking account at your local bank. You want to get information from a couple of banks and look for the best product. Your parent is equally responsible for any action that occurs on that personal checking account because they signed as a co-signer.

If your parent co-signs for a car loan or mortgage, then they are equally responsible for making sure the debt gets paid on time. Co-signing for anything is the same as though you signed up yourself. You are equally responsible.

I meet a lot of parents who co-sign for car and bank loans for their kids. The kids lose a job and do not understand the importance of paying bills on time and both parties get bad credit. The parents decide that they need to consolidate their own debt. Not realizing their FICO score has plummeted because the child always paid their joint debt **late**, the parents get declined.

You need to make sure that you think very hard before you co-sign any debt for any child, family members or friends. When you sign on the dotted line, the lender does not care that you are only the co-signer, you are also on the hook for making timely payments and making sure the whole debt is paid in full. Many people will say that I am only the co-signer and don't understand why their credit was affected. The lender asked for a co-signer for a reason. The main reason is the applicant, whether it is a child or friend, may not have bad credit while applying alone, they just have no credit. The co-signer offers the lender more security and better chance of repayment if the applicant defaults on the loan.

Life Lesson: *Understand you are responsible for all debt as a co-signer.*

If your child turns eighteen then they can apply for their own credit card and open their own personal checking account. I like to open the first checking account with my child at sixteen and act as the co-signer. I will go over the bank statements every month with the child, educating him on how to properly maintain it. I will make sure that they use the debit card, which usually comes with the checking account properly, and help them to record everything in their checking account register. I open the checking account first in my name and apply for 1,000 dollars overdraft protection. Once the approval is in place, I then add my child to the bank accounts as a second signer and they get the benefits of an account that now has overdraft protection established.

You want to try and find a personal checking account that has no monthly maintenance fees. A debit card looks like a credit card and it has the master card logo on it. It can be used like a credit card. The only difference is the money comes out of your checking account electronically at the point of sale, instead of getting a bill and having thirty days to pay the bill.

Life Lesson: *While using a debit card at any point of sale always select the credit button and you will avoid a debit POS bank fee.*

You always want to make sure that you have enough money in your personal checking account prior to using this debit card because the money will come out electronically to pay that merchant where you used the debit card that day. You can also get cash from your personal checking account at the ATM by using this debit card.

If you use the debit card and don't have the funds in your checking account to pay, you will be charged an overdraft fee from the bank and still owe that money to the merchant.

These overdraft fees will begin to add up and if you make this same mistake continually, you will begin to incur a lot of bank fees.

Life Lesson: *Overdraft protection on a checking account will help to avoid bank fees so try to get that in place after you open a new checking account.*

When a bank customer begins to show a pattern of consistently overdrawing their personal checking account your bank may request that you pay off all the bank fees and they can close out your account. People who are always overdrawn on their personal checking account, otherwise known as bouncing a check, become a risk to the bank by taking a possible loss on you.

Banks do not like taking a loss and then they will close out your account. If you are unable to pay back the bank for using a debit card or you wrote bad checks to people and did not have the money in the checking account to cover, then the bank will have to charge off your account.

The bank will then report you to the credit bureau indicating the loss that they took on your abuse of the personal checking account. Any negative reports to your credit bureau will drive down your FICO score. You will then receive collection calls from the bank, trying to track you down to pay for those items that you purchased with your debit card.

If you purposely write checks with no money in the account, it is considered bank fraud. The person that you wrote a bad check to can report you to the police and you could be arrested for what they call bad check writing. You don't want to get in trouble with the police, so make sure that you have enough money in your personal checking account prior to writing out checks and using your debit card.

You do not have to accept the debit card when you open up a new personal checking account. It is your choice but I recommend that you get a debit card. They offer a convenience to you when getting money at the ATM, purchasing gas and groceries. The debit cards can also be used like a credit card, so if you are ever stranded and need to rent a car or get a hotel room in an emergency then use the debit card.

Life Lesson: *Spend some time with your local bank to learn all about the advantages and disadvantages of a personal checking account and debit card.*

I know it sounds like a lot of work maintaining a personal checking account, but it is not. Make sure that you write down in your checking account register all of your bank deposits and all of the checks that you wrote. You also want to keep the receipts for all the debit card purchases that you made and record them in this register that same day because those are the electronic checks that you wrote.

Life Lesson: *Become a responsible person and manage your checking account properly. Make sure to record all debit card purchases made daily into your checking account register.*

People get into trouble using the debit cards because they **forget** to get the receipt and write it down in the checking account register. They now lost track of exactly how much money that they have available in the checking account. You will get a monthly checking account statement and you want to reconcile this with your checking account register.

You can also go online and review your checking account balances daily and this will list all of your debit card purchases. If you lose a receipt you can take the information from your account online and record it in the checking account register.

The key to maintaining a good personal checking account is to make sure that you have the correct balance showing in your checking account register prior to using a debit card and writing a check to somebody. I have had the same personal checking account for twenty-five years and monitor the activity daily with on-line banking.

A personal checking account is something that we all will need and you should have. You can also have your monthly paycheck electronically deposited into your personal checking account every pay period. We call this procedure direct deposit and I highly recommend that you set this up with your employer.

You will actually get your money electronically deposited into your account faster than if you wait to get the payroll checks from your employer. If you are supposed to be paid every Friday and you set up direct deposit then your money is sent via **ACH**, which is an electronic deposit on midnight Thursday the day before.

If you wait for you payroll check then you have to sign the back of it, wait in line at the bank and make the deposit manually with a bank teller. This direct deposit saves you a lot of time and money because your money is available much faster and safer through ACH directly into your personal checking account.

Once you graduate from college and get a job, then you should start to build your credit score even higher. To build a good credit and drive up the FICO score, you will need to use credit and pay the balance off in full every month. You can also make monthly payments prior to the due date and that will also help drive up your score. **I recommend paying credit bills off in full every month.**

Life Lesson: *Set up direct deposit from your employer, it is safer, and it will speed up the process for you to get that take home net pay into your checking account.*

Your debit card, even though you can use it as a credit card, will not help to increase your FICO score because you don't receive a monthly bill. Banks don't report these good transactions to the bureaus because debit card payments electronically come out of your checking account. Remember that banks will report misuse of a personal checking account to the credit bureau, if the bank takes a loss on you. The debit card is a primary reason people get into trouble with the checking account, because they forget to record the transactions.

Another way to establish credit and begin to increase your FICO score is to apply for a department store card from a favorite store in the mall where you like to shop, such as American Eagle. Since you already had that one pre- approved credit card from college, you should be able to qualify for this department store card with a small lending limit. You will then use the department store card when you purchase items at this store. You can pay that bill off in full each month and this will get a favorable reporting to the credit bureau on your behalf.

You can still use the pre-approved credit card that you got in college for any purchases where MasterCard or Visa is accepted. You pay that monthly credit card bill in full every month. You are now using these two cards one is the department store card and the other is the Master or Visa card to help build up that FICO score. The more you use those two cards and pay those bills prior to the due date, the higher your FICO score will go up.

While visiting the dealership, if you want to purchase a new car they have several finance options. Some local banks, along with the finance arm of the manufacturer, will offer you options to finance a new car. The manufacturer finance company usually has a first time buyer program for college graduates. They are more willing to lend you the money knowing that you don't have a bad credit history, just a new limited one.

You want to finance the car so you now have a third lending experience on file. You will receive a coupon payment book which tells you how much your monthly payment is and when it is due each month. Make sure that you allow enough time to mail all your payments in and this will also help that FICO score increase.

You can also set up a direct payment plan from your new personal checking account to the lender who financed your new car. This electronic payment system is great because you will never be late mailing your car payment in, as the bill payment will come out of the personal checking account automatically on the due date you enter in the computer.

You can have direct deposit from your paycheck into the personal checking account and then have direct payment to the lender for your car payments. Make sure you are recording both transactions in your personal checking account register and it will all work efficiently on your behalf.

Life Lesson: *Once you're working full time start to build your credit score and establish yourself as a low risk to any lending institution.*

You are now on your way to building up a high FICO credit score and maintaining a personal checking account. The main purpose in building that high FICO score is to help you one day make the largest purchase you will ever make, which is a **home**. Before a bank will offer you a mortgage, they will check your credit bureau file, FICO score and also the way you maintain your personal checking account. You may qualify if everything looks good and you have a twenty percent down payment for the home.

Life Lesson: *Just like building blocks, we are on track to building your financial future.*

After you get your drivers license, one credit card, personal checking and savings account you want to write down all the account numbers and keep them in a safe place. You also want to write down the toll-free customer service phone numbers that come with all your accounts. If you lose any of these items or worse yet, your wallet gets stolen and the credit card is gone, it is important to have the 16 digit account number and phone number located on the back of the credit card, so that you can report it stolen or lost. Planning ahead will save you time and money by reporting the incident right away.

These are just a few fatherly advice tips to help any young adult begin their life in finance. We need to understand about debt and ways to control our spending habits. We need to understand that there are two types of debt. The first is what they call **constructive debt** when used to acquire assets that are going up in value and we are allowed to write off the interest payments on our tax returns. This type of debt currently includes your house mortgage interest and a home equity loan. In years past the government used to allow other interest debt payments, but took them away.

Constructive debt would also be considered good debt because writing off interest on your taxes helps to lower your overall tax burden, which can save you money. This mortgage debt also meant that once the mortgage was paid in full you owned the house free and clear. Your house is the biggest and most important debt that you will acquire. Any debt, such as a mortgage, is good because over time your home will increase in value and hopefully be worth more thirty years from now. This is what they also call an asset that appreciates over time. This is a good thing and why it is considered constructive debt.

Destructive debt is borrowing money for assets that will be going down in value immediately after you purchase it. This other debt that you may incur will not allow you to write off interest payments either on your tax returns. This type of debt is primarily credit card and car loan debt. Credit card debt does not appreciate in value like a home that you own; therefore it is considered destructive. Car loans can be considered destructive because once you drive that new car off the lot it depreciates in value by almost fifty percent and you can't write off that interest on your tax returns. We need a car to travel to and from work so it is important and certain cars do appreciate in value, especially my dream car the Chevrolet Corvette Convertible. So, I would consider them an asset and necessity, just like a home. We all love our cars and they provide us with positive energy. We lose out on writing off the interest on our tax returns.

I would not get to caught up in what is constructive or destructive debt. I would try to focus more of my attention on trying to control my spending habits and understand that we have to fulfill our needs first prior to satisfying all of our wants. It is very easy to get into credit card debt and you can always find help with your parents or local bank manager. Your bank can be a viable resource for you and you can learn much by visiting with them as the banking relationship grows.

Life Lesson: *We all will experience debt at some point in our life, so appreciate the benefits and try to control it at all times. If your debt is getting out of control then use all the resources available to you and ask for help.*

I want to thank all of you for reading my book. I hope my **Fatherly Advice** and at least one **Life Lesson** can make your life better. I wish you all the positive energy, confidence to succeed in the classroom, athletic fields and win in the game of life. Remember that the four C's **C**onfidence, **C**ourage, **C**ompetitiveness, and **C**ontinued improvement can be applied to help you reach your goals in school, sports, work, and life.

If you are presently in credit card debt and you would like to put a plan together to get out of debt. I suggest that you look at my goal setting workshop page in the extra innings section of this book. Set a good S.M.A.R.T goal and follow the plan until you have reached your goal to get out of debt.

I suggest that you also read building dynamic credit in the extra innings section of this book for more detailed information about debt and building a great FICO score. All of the information listed under the extra innings section of this book is great best practices to help any young adult or parent meet their goals and succeed in life.

Life Lesson: *Money can't buy happiness, and health. Understand and respect the power of money and debt as it affects the way we all live but don't let it change who you are and the greatness you bring to this world.*

Extra Innings

Sample of a Monthly Budget Form:

1. Total Monthly Net pay: (After taxes, health insurance 401-k, etc.)
   Some employers may pay the following ways:
   a. Weekly: $_____
   b. Bi- Monthly: $_____
   c. Monthly: $_____

   Total Monthly **Net Pay**: $_____

   <u>Monthly Bills amount owed:</u>

   1. Car Payment: $_____
   2. Car Insurance: $_____
   3. Car Excise Tax: This is annual expense charged by the town where you garage the car: $_____
   4. Gas to run the car $_____: budget your monthly expense to operate the car.
   5. Rent: $_____
   6. Rental Insurance: $_____

7. Mortgage payment if you own a home: $_____
8. Home Insurance if you own a home: $_____
9. Property Taxes if you own the home: $_____
10. Credit Card bill: $_____ try to pay balance off in full every month.
11. Electric Bill: $_____
12. Gas/ Oil Bill $_____ to heat Your Home
13. Cell Phone $_____
14. Home Phone: $_____
15. Cable TV bill: $_____
16. Groceries, Lunches, Daily Coffee, Meals out, Prescriptions, Church, etc: $_____

Total Monthly **Bills**: $_____

Your Monthly Surplus or Shortage: $_____
(This is your spendable income minus your total expenses, it is your fun money left over)

You can create your own monthly budget style. You can break out all your monthly bills in categories. For example:

1. Housing:
2. Car Expenses:
3. Utilities:
4. Credit cards:
5. Miscellaneous:
6. Investments:

Extra Innings

Instructions to Balance Your Checkbook:

It is important that you balance your checkbook every month so that your records match the banks records. We all know that your bank can make a mistake but it is more likely that you have a math error in your checkbook register.

Follow these steps to balance your **bank statement** to your **checkbook register**.

1. Make sure you are logging all of your financial transactions in your checking account register including checks that you have written, atm withdrawals, debit card purchases. A good practice is put all atm and debit card receipts in your pocket and each night record them in the register making sure to keep all bank deposit slips and receipts forever.

2. Your bank statement may arrive in the mail or if you are environmentally green in you signed up for this service with your bank then your statement will be sent to you online. **Reconcile your checks** by looking at the bank statement for each check that you wrote and then placing a check mark in your register next to that check that corresponds with your bank statement.

3. **Reconcile your deposits** by doing the same as step 2 above making sure each cash deposit, check deposit or direct payroll deposit is matched with your bank statement to your register. You can place a check mark in the register next to each deposit that corresponds with your bank statement.

4. **Reconcile your ATM withdrawals and Debit Card purchases** by doing the same step 2 above making sure all atm withdrawals, and debit card purchases match your bank statement to your register. You can place a check mark in the register next to each withdrawal that corresponds with your bank statement.

5. **Record interest earned and bank fees** from your bank statement and apply it to your register. Interest earned will be a credit in your ledger and bank fees are recorded as a debit. Check your bank statement for any other bank fees and make sure that you record them in your checkbook register as a debit.

6. **Take out a blank piece of paper** and write two headings on the top. The left side titles **all outstanding checks** and on the right side **all outstanding deposits.**

7. Find all outstanding checks that appear in your register, atm withdrawals, and debit card purchases that you did not place a check mark next to. (These will not appear on your monthly bank statement because they occurred after your bank statement was printed for that month.) Total these up under all outstanding checks.

8. Find all outstanding deposits by going through your checkbook register for any that do not appear on your monthly bank statement. Total these up under all outstanding deposits.

9. **Record your banks statement ending balance** and add that to your all-outstanding deposits column.

10. **Calculate your balance** by taking all your outstanding deposits column and subtract that from all your outstanding checks column and that figure should equal the figure that

Nine Innings

you have shown as your ending balance in your checkbook register.

Extra Innings

Goal Setting Workshop:

I believe that it is important for us to continue to challenge ourselves and not get complacent. When we become complacent in our life it leads to laziness. Setting goals can be short, mid and long term. Setting goals will help keep you focused and challenged as you strive to reach and attain those goals that you set. Writing your goals down will make it much more likely that you will succeed. **Plan your work and work your plan.**

You dream of a project and now you must plan that project and turn all of your attention to develop a result oriented goal that will enable you to be successful. Goals should be **SMART**- specific, measurable, attainable, realistic and timely. This acronym **SMART** has a number of different variations, which can be used to help keep you focus while supporting your efforts for setting a goal and then working towards achieving it with success.

S-specific: Do you know exactly what you want to accomplish with details?

M-measurable: Can you access and measure your progress for that goal?

A-attainable: Given your situation can your goal be reached?

R-realistic: Do you have the ability to make the dream and goal you set come true.

T-timely: What is the desired time frame to complete the project that you have set.

The next time that you decide on a project take a moment to consider whether your goal is **SMART**. Follow the above guidelines and it will help you focus and succeed.

For a bad example: My project or goal is "I want to write this book." It was a dream of mine but I did not make it a **SMART** goal and follow any of the steps listed above.

For a good example: My project is I want to write a book to share all my life lessons learned to educate my two sons helping to keep them safe, I would like it to be at least 100 pages in length, and have the project completed by my forty fifth birthday on September 21, 2010. I will commit to writing one page every night after work taking my time until I finish the book.

This good example is more detailed and it is **SMART** that clearly states a specific, measurable, attainable, realistic and timely goal for completing my project and achieving a dream of mine. It was important for me not to put any extra pressure on myself by setting an aggressive completion date but a realistic one that I could attain by working on the project each night writing one page at a time until completion.

Setting goals is all about you deciding that you want to accomplish something then it involves you to figure out and set a plan in place on exactly what you need to do to get where you want to go and how long it will take for you to get there. The **SMART** acronym is the fundamental building blocks and process to help fit your needs and make your project or dream a success and reality.

Extra Innings

Building Dynamic Credit:

I believe that is important for all of us to become financially independent, but learning how to do it can be a challenge. Building good credit is a must because it will help you qualify for loans, credit cards, car loans, car insurance, cell phone plans, rental applications, and directly affect whether you get a job. The Higher your FICO credit score is the less risk you are to lenders, landlords, employers, insurance companies and you will qualify for better rates and terms. One seemingly minor misstep such as late payments, and maxing out your credit cards can drive down your FICO score.

If you're just starting out, you have a once in a lifetime opportunity to build a great credit history the right way, which will benefit you once you apply for that first mortgage on your new house. Here are nine helpful ways to get you started on the path to financial independence and the best advice for everyone is to always stay responsible while you understand the importance of your credit as you build up a good score and try to maintain it during your journey through life.

1. **Establish a checking and savings account**: Lenders view bank accounts as a sign of stability, once your child turns sixteen and gets their license, I recommend that one parent who has excellent credit open the accounts first in the parents name only. The parent then should apply for overdraft

protection of $1,000 dollars on the checking account and make sure that it is established on the account prior to adding the child on as a second signer of the account. Now the child is placed as a second signer to the established accounts and you now have a joint account with overdraft protection in place. The overdraft protection will help in the event the account becomes overdrawn and together you can work with the child to maintain a good relationship with the bank. Set up on-line banking.

2. **Check your credit report**: It is important to find out what if anything lenders are saying about you in your credit report at each of the three major credit bureaus such as Equifax, Experian, and Trans Union. You can get one free report from all three each year at *annualcreditreport.com* Credit reports are used to create your credit scores, the three digit numbers that lenders will typically use to gauge your creditworthiness and risk as a customer to repay the loan your applying for. Checking your credit reports for accuracy either through a credit bureau mistake or identity theft can affect your score drastically and lower your score.

3. **The basics of credit scoring:** The two most important factors in your FICO score are whether you pay your bills on time and how much of your available credit you actually use. It is crucial that you pay all your bills on time. Set up automatic bill payments with your online banking or a reminder system, so that you're never late. Make sure that you never max out the limits of any of your credit cards or even get close. Try to keep your credit use to less than 15% of your credit limit which will help drive up your FICO score and prevent you from getting in over your head in debt. You don't need to carry a balance on a credit card to have good credit scores. Paying your bill in full each month is the best way to keep your finances in shape and build up your credit all at the same time.

4. **Piggyback on your parent's good credit:** The fastest way to establish a great credit history is to borrow your

parents record by being added to a credit card as a joint account holder. If your father adds you to his credit card then the credit history of the father with that account can be imported to your credit bureau file giving you an instant credit record. If you father has handled the account well, that reflects well on you. If he has not and has mistakes such as any late payments or other problems then those become your mistakes as well and can hurt your chances to get future credit. I only recommend this for somebody who has strong credit before you add your child. You should have a 730 FICO score or higher.

5. **Establish your own credit:** You want to establish a good mix of credit such as a major credit card with Visa, MasterCard, Discover, or American Express, Gas credit card, Department store credit card, Auto Installment loan, or Mortgage. Visa and MasterCard are most widely accepted by the merchant and you want to make sure you get a card with no annual fee, rewards, and the lowest rate possible. I recommend that you pay the balance off in full each month then the rate is irrelevant.

6. **Take Advantage of one-pre-approved Credit card**: Once you turn eighteen and you receive an offer that indicates that you are pre approved for a major credit card such as Visa or MasterCard, I recommend that you take advantage of the offer. They usually do not require any income verification, job employment, and it is a great way to get that first major credit card established.

7. **Don't apply for several credit cards at one time:** Now that you have established credit in your own name don't go wild. If you apply for too much credit in too short a period of time your credit score will fall. Every time you fill out a credit application that lender will look at your credit report and this will create what they call a *credit inquiry* on your report. If you have more then five-credit inquiries from just credit card companies in one month then your score can

fall. You only need one major credit card as outlined in this book.

8. **Open a mad money savings account:** Mad money is also known as your rainy day fund, or emergency savings account. A good rule of thumb is to have at least six months of savings set aside in the event that you lose your job and have no monthly income coming in. This account will be used to keep making those monthly payments on time so you are prepared to protect the good credit score that you have worked so hard building up.

9. **The Closer and I don't mean baseball:** Some people think that they can improve their credit score by closing out credit accounts that they may not be using. This can actually have a reverse effect and drive down your score because credit-reporting agencies look at the length of time you have had any particular credit open. The FICO score is calculated and weighted in five ways.
    a. Your payment history represents 35%
    b. Dollar Amounts owed represents 30%
    c. Length of time for each credit established represents 15%
    d. New Credit issued represents 10%
    e. Types of credit applied such as revolving (credit card), installment (car loan) represents 10%.

Extra Innings

Financial Investment Guide:

Every aspect of your life is influenced by money where you live, your house, car, the food we eat, the clothes we wear, the work that we do, our friends, and the number of children that you may have, are a direct result of our relationship with money. We need to start thinking about money like you would any of the people that you spend your time with. We should respect and recognize the importance of money and the power that it brings to our lives and the attention that it deserves from us and striking a balance not allowing money to change your family values and who you really are as a person. Having a healthy relationship with money, a spouse, child, parent, friend can sometimes be frustrating, but we listen and try to learn from any mistake then improve the situation.

In school they don't teach us about money or the affects that is has on our feelings, which can be viewed as either a negative or positive relationship. Our parents have all said Money doesn't grow on trees, Money is the root of all evil, and it takes Money to make Money. These statements can influence the way our children view money as something negative and therefore we grow up to believe that having a lot of Money is not in the cards for us. I say that it is possible for all of you to have Money and you should not be afraid to go out and be successful making as much Money as you can. Once you do then just like a child you want to protect it, invest it so it will grow, and share it with your family and the less fortunate living your life to the fullest.

1. **To retire rich**, you need to start saving now. The sooner that you begin to start investing your money the longer time you will have for it to compound and grow. If you want to have one million dollars saved by the age of 65 and your able to earn 8% return per year then consider this. A 25-year-old person needs to make an annual investment of $3,900 and a 45 year old would have to invest $21,900 to reach that same goal at the age of 65. The younger person started 20 years sooner and had all that time for his money to compound and the older person who *procrastinated* needed to catch up and invest much more to reach that same goal.

2. **Max out your 401-k:** Once you begin to work full time and you review your benefits and if your employers offer a 401-k retirement savings plan you want to take the maximum allowed out of your paycheck to invest. Some employers will also match up to your investment a certain percentage. This is beneficial to you in many ways. One your money grows tax deferred and you don't pay taxes until you begin to take it out in retirement. Second you may receive a company match, and that is like free money. Third your investment will reduce your tax burden every year that you participate and most importantly the compound effect of that money growing over time just like item 1 above.

3. **Set up a traditional or Roth IRA: IRA stands for Individual retirement Account.** If you have completed step 2 above and have extra money left over then look into setting up a Traditional or Roth IRA and fund that every year. The amount of your annual income will determine which one of these investment products you can use and both forms of the IRA are great ways to save for retirement although each offers different advantages. Google to learn more.

4. **Invest small amounts monthly:** You can set up automatic investment from your checking account into your mutual

funds each month for as low as $100 dollars per month. This is a great way for you to become disciplined and not spend that money on things that you really don't need and you won't miss the money if it automatically comes out of your checkbook each month. Make sure that you have it in your budget and can afford making this commitment. This form of investing is called **Dollar Cost Averaging.** Your money is buying shares at different price levels each month and as the price of the mutual fund shares fluctuate you maybe buying more or less shares every month but over the course of a year your average is good. Invest $100 per month earning 8% return and after 10 years you could have $18,295; 20 years $58,902; 30 years $149,076; 40 years $349,101. That is the power of compounding and time with just a small monthly investment of 100 dollars per month. *Are you excited yet, I am.*

5. **Invest in the right mutual fund to match your goals:** We need to identify your investment goals, such as retirement, Childs education, purchase a home, etc. You need to understand that your time horizon to reach these goals will dictate which type of investment product you will need to best meet those needs and goals. Short-term goals such as to purchase a home in three years you will want to stay conservative and use bank products that are FDIC insured like a bank CD, or money market account. Retirement or college long-term goals with a 10, or 15-year time horizon then consider growth mutual funds, which over this time frame offer the best returns, but they are not FDIC insured. Remember that asset allocation is the process of deciding how your portfolio will be spread across different kinds of investments such as stocks, bonds, and mutual funds.

6. **How much do you have to invest:** We need to look at our monthly budget to determine the amount that we are comfortable to invest each month to reach these goals. Take a good look at your monthly spending, your monthly income, and then do the math to figure out how much you will need to invest to make your goal a reality.

7. **Stay the Course:** Once you have taken the time to set the goal, check your budget and determine how much you can afford each month and chosen the right investment portfolio then stay disciplined and make sure you execute the plan. We now need to set up the investment accounts and have the money your able to afford automatically coming out of your checking account and directly investing into the mutual fund that you decide will meet your goals. *"Lets getter done."*

I hope that you find all the wealth and happiness on your journey to financial freedom.

You can always contact your local bank and request a meeting with the financial consultation and get their expert advice. You can contact mutual fund companies directly and research those funds and do it yourself. The most popular and cost effective mutual fund families are Vanguard, T. Rowe Price, Janus, and Fidelity.

Extra Innings

Financial Documents Archive Checklist:

The following are a list of important financial documents to help keep you organized and best practices that I have used as a financial advisor for over twenty years. I will offer you a time frame for holding certain personal documents before you decide to destroy any records. These items should be kept in a safe that will not burn in the event you ever have a fire in your home and these documents will be protected.

Personal Documents:
1. ***Your birth certificate***- Keep the original for you and your loved ones in a safe forever. Make a copy of each when you need them to conduct business.
2. ***Drivers License***- Make a copy of both sides and write down customer service number if ever lost. Having a copy will help you get a replacement faster.
3. ***Passport***- I recommend that you and your loved ones get a passport and they are usually good for 10 years before you will renew. You will need one for travel out of the United States and you can apply for them now at your local town hall where you live.

4. ***Marriage Certificate-*** Keep original in a safe and make a copy especially for woman who may need copies to change bank records as they make a name change once they take on a husband's last name.
5. ***Death Certificate-*** I hope you will not need these anytime soon but be prepared and keep original in the safe on a loved one and make copies for all financial institutions to change bank records.
6. ***Credit Cards-*** make a photocopy of both sides along with the customer service numbers in the event they are lost or stolen. Make sure that you review your credit card statements each month for accuracy and your not double billed for the same item.
7. ***Divorce Best Practice-*** Cancel and close out any joint credit cards and bank accounts in the event of a divorce before your spouse begins to start charging up items that you are not willing to help pay. This will help to protect your credit score.
8. ***Credit Report-*** Make sure that you review your credit report at least once per year and that is free to check for accuracy. If any mistakes then write a letter to all three bureaus and keep copy for your records until it is resolved and corrected.
9. ***Other-*** any other important personal documents, Divorce Decree, Prenuptial or Postnuptial agreements, adoption certificates, etc keep forever.
10. ***Tax Returns-*** Make sure it is accurate before you sign off on them. Keep for seven years to be on the safe side along with all receipts that you use as a write off such as medical, charities, travel and entertainment expenses, mortgage interest, real estate property taxes, etc.
11. ***Investment documentation-*** Keep forever your trade confirmations paperwork for your annual contribution to a Roth or Traditional IRA's. It could be thirty years or longer

before you begin to make withdrawals and you may need these records.

12. ***Paid in full Loans*-** Keep all auto, home, and school loans that you have paid in full for at least seven years.

13. ***House and stock sales*-** keep all records of any stocks or homes that you sell. You will have to pay capital gains taxes and will need these records to help determine your capital gains that you earned on the investments when completing your tax returns. If you own a home for two years and then sell it your capital gains tax presently is lower then if you sold that house prior to the two-year time frame.

14. ***House Records*-** Keep all information with regards to your home in the safe such as the Deed, Promissory notes, Insurance on contents, fire, and flood, copy of title insurance, and appraisals you had done to protect any valuable items stored in your house like jewelry, art, autograph sports memorabilia, antiques, forever.

15. ***Insurance*-** all insurance policies for your cars, boats, house, recreational vehicles, and personal life insurance. Any titles proving ownership of these items should be kept in your safe until you sell them.

16. ***Social Security*-** Keep your original social security card, and loved ones, in your safe and make a copy for any financial institution who may require to view it. Protect these to avoid identity theft. We receive an annual social security statement, so make sure it is accurate and your gross personal annual income from your w'2s is properly reported. This will help with social security benefits later in life. If any mistakes are found then contact the social security customer service and get corrected. Keep in your safe forever.

17. ***Set up your Last Will and Testament*-** You need at least this to make sure that you instruct where all your assets will go to the proper loved ones upon your death.

18. ***Estate Planning***- If your net worth is over one million dollars and you own a home, have kids then you should speak with a financial advisor to have these additional items set up on your behalf to protect all your assets and avoid probate court which can be very expensive. If you die, you want to make sure that your loved ones are protected and these estate documents can help avoid probate court and costly fees associated with that process. ***Advanced directive*** and ***durable power of attorney for health care, financial durable power of attorney, Revocable living trust***, and ***a pour over will.***

Make sure that your family knows where these documents are located in the event of an unexpected accident or death while your traveling. A little preparation and organization of these important documents will go a long way to help you and your family later.

Extra Innings

Acknowledgments:

There is an old saying that behind the success of any man you will find the true strength and success, which is a woman. For me, that is my beautiful, loving and faithful wife Susanne. I want to thank you for all your support over the years and for your confidence in helping me write this book. Our first twenty-four years together have been wonderful and I look forward to spending the rest of my life with you.

Susanne, you are an amazing woman with strong faith and you have done a brilliant job raising our two sons Jacob and Joshua. I love you. I thank Jacob and Joshua for reminding me daily what matters most in this world and it is having both of you. If at any point in time I feel down and out with stress that pops up in my life and work, I simply think of you both and it instantly disappears. You bring that much joy into my life and my love for you both is unconditional.

My inspiration for writing this book came from Jacob and Joshua as I strive to be a better father and share my trials and tribulations during my life's journey to happiness and bliss. This book is a guide for both of you to reflect on and hopefully learn from my mistakes and improve upon your life. As always, remain positive and have confidence in all that you do. I love you both and remember to always take care of each other and your mother.

To my loving and caring parents who both sacrificed so much starting their family at such a young age – your love and support during my youth is much appreciated. I don't think I would have ever made it through those years without both of you guiding and counseling me.

To my sisters Janene and Melissa who are both strong willed, beautiful, intelligent and caring – I love and thank you both for always being they're for me. To my younger brother Michael who is a caring and a loveable person, I thank you for always being by my side. I am your biggest fan and want you to know that I love you very much and need for you to start believing in yourself. Mike, enjoy life and begin the journey to peace and happiness.

To Dr. John Carnes Walton who was my high school English teacher – You are a true inspiration and remarkable person. You have shared your wisdom and knowledge with me over the past twenty-five years and never missed sending me a birthday card. My wife, family and I appreciate your friendship, guidance and support all the time. You're a great educator, brilliant, and best friend anyone could ever hope to have. **Thank You.**

To Robert Perreault my high school guidance counselor – You never gave up on me, especially when I had failed in my duties as a student. Out of the hundreds of kids that you were responsible to guide and prepare for college, you saw something in me that I did not at the time. You believed that I could go to college and succeed. Thank You.

Thank you to my Aunt Marie and Uncle Dr. Jack Klie – I appreciate all the excellent health care you have provided to my family and me for the past twenty-five years. The both of you helped save my dad's life when he fell ill this past year. Every American should receive the kind of health care that I got from you Jack. I love you both.

To my Aunt Sheila and Uncle Ronny – I appreciate all your love and support over the years and the good times that we spent together as a family. I love you both.

To my brothers- in-law Paul and Pete – I appreciate all your love that you provide to my sisters and thank you for taking care of them and my nieces and nephews. I love you both. Paul, you are the older brother that I never had and appreciate all the fun times we shared together.

To my nephews Kyle, Sean, Matt, and Aiden – Uncle Lenny is very proud of you all and I look forward to watching you all grow and

Nine Innings

succeed in life. To Shayleigh, my parent's first granddaughter, we look forward to spoiling and protecting you, as you get older. I love you all.

To everyone on my wife's side of the family – I thank you all for accepting me into your family and supporting us as we raise our family together. To my mother-in-law Minnie and father-in-law William – I appreciate all that you have done by raising such a wonderful daughter Susanne.

To Chris Head, whom I met in the sixth grade and is my best friend – We have great memories growing up together and meeting our wives, who were and still are best friends today. We have remained best friends all this time and now get to enjoy watching all of our children grow up.

To all my friends who visit Lenny's Pub – I cherish all the memories and good times we have shared together. I appreciate all your support and friendship over the years and look forward to spending many more. Chris Lima a true and trusted friend forever.

Most of all I wish to thank God and his son Jesus for giving me the strength and guidance in my life. I have been so blessed with many gifts, and it is the Holy Spirit who helps keep me strong as I continue my journey through life.

I have dedicated the rest of my life to reaching out to any child in my community who needs a mentor and a shoulder to lean on during any difficult time he or she may be experiencing. Paying it forward, as they say, is just that, sharing your knowledge and experience with others who may benefit from it. I believe that our children are the future and we need to reach out and help them find their way in life.

This book is for my sons Jacob and Joshua. All the young men, woman, and parents who find a life lesson that helps give them strength, knowledge, wisdom, and success.

In Loving Memory of my grandparents:
Harold and Viola Gaynor
William and Anna Silva
Mother in Law- Minnie Hughes
A beautiful poem written by my cousin Lisa Zeppa
My Grandmother's last day

My love to Vavoa'
I visited my grandmother and didn't know that was it
There was more I wanted to tell her I have to admit

I looked in her eyes and saw nothing at all
The color had changed they were shallow and small

Somehow she seemed to know my presence was there
Maybe that is just what I hoped for as I looked at her blank stare

I am grateful I saw her the very last day
Before the angels and saints took my Vavoa' away

I'll remember her stories and how she made us laugh at everything
I'll remember the Christmas' she joined us and we would all sing

She was a very strong woman my dad always told me
She took care of many both friends and family

I hope she is in a place where she has finally found rest
A place full of peace and beauty... simply the best

She leaves behind her children my dad being one
He is the strength of my family she should be proud of this son

I am so proud he sat by her as she passed from this earth
It only shows me deeper what his presence is worth

A man of his word he was there at the end
Holding the hand of his mother leading her to a new friend

That friend would be Jesus, the Lord of all light
My dad wanted to be there he fled to her in the middle of the night

As he watched her slip away he knew this wasn't the end
Both he and his mother knew they would see each other again

God bless my grandmother may her soul rise above
May we all be blessed with God's spirit of goodness and love.

A special thank you to Kathy Buck for taking her time to edit this book. I cherish our friendship along with your husband Jeff, your sister Michelle and her husband Richard Silva. I treasure your mom Carolyn and miss your dad Dan everyday, whom I was proud to call my friend.

I love you all and appreciate your support while writing this book

Playoffs

About the Author

Lenny Silva is married for eighteen years and a father of two boys. He has a passion for baseball and finished with a Hall of Fame collegiate career. He is a coach and trusted mentor to young adults in his community. He has twenty-three years experience as a licensed financial advisor.

Made in the USA
Middletown, DE
30 July 2019